EVENTS THAT
CHANGED THE
WORLD

1860–1880

═══The Nineteenth Century═══

EVENTS THAT CHANGED THE WORLD

1860–1880

═══ The Nineteenth Century ═══

**Other books in the
Events That Changed the World series:**

The Nineteenth Century
1800–1820
1820–1840
1840–1860
1880–1900

The Twentieth Century
1900–1920
1920–1940
1940–1960
1960–1980
1980–2000

EVENTS THAT CHANGED THE WORLD

1860–1880

=The Nineteenth Century=

Kelly Doyle, *Book Editor*

Bruce Glassman, *Vice President*
Bonnie Szumski, *Publisher*
Helen Cothran, *Managing Editor*

GREENHAVEN PRESS
An imprint of Thomson Gale, a part of The Thomson Corporation

Detroit • New York • San Francisco • San Diego • New Haven, Conn.
Waterville, Maine • London • Munich

LIBRARY OF CONGRESS CATALOGING-IN-PUBLICATION DATA

1860–1880 / Kelly Doyle, book editor.
 p. cm. — (Events that changed the world)
 Includes bibliographical references and index.
 ISBN 0-7377-2035-2 (lib. bdg. : alk. paper)
  1. History, Modern—19th century. 2. History, Modern—19th century—Sources.
 I. Doyle, Kelly. II. Series.
 D358.A14 2005
 909.81—dc22   2004042443

Printed in the United States of America

CONTENTS

major impact on the course of the Civil War and the future of America.

Event 3: The First Labor Union Changes the World Economy: 1864

1. Address and Provisional Rules of the International Working Men's Association
The establishment of the International Working Men's Association in London marked the beginning of a new kind of trade unionism whose influences are widely established today all over the world.

Event 4: Lee Surrenders at Appomattox and Ends the Civil War: 1865

1. The Night Before Appomattox
Confederate general George Edward Pickett wrote this letter to his wife on the eve of the surrender of Union forces at Appomattox, Virginia, in April 1865.

2. The Road to Reunion
By the spring of 1865 the Confederate army had been punished beyond measure. Lee's surrender to Union general Ulysses S. Grant at the Appomattox Court House ended the American Civil War.

Event 5: The Siege of Paris Gives Rise to the First Proletariat Government: 1871

1. The Rise of the Paris Commune Signals Future Violent Revolution
The Paris Commune ended the most ferocious

outbreak of civil violence in nineteenth-century Europe and is still a subject of intense historical interest and controversy.

Event 6: The First Impressionist Art Exhibit: 1874

Event 7: The Battle of the Little Bighorn: 1876

changed not only the science of medicine but also the way medicine was practiced.

2. The Germ Theory and Its Applications to Medicine and Surgery

In this paper delivered to the French Academy of Sciences on April 29, 1878, Louis Pasteur outlines the principles of the germ theory and its applications in medicine and surgery.

Event 10: Queen Victoria Is Made Empress of India: 1877

1. The End of Empire

In January 1877 the prime minister of England, Benjamin Disraeli, altered the queen's title from "queen of India" to that of "queen empress of India." The appointment had symbolic significance and repercussions on the rest of the world.

Event 11: Porfirio Díaz Is Elected President of Mexico: 1877

1. The Making of a Dictator

Porfirio Díaz came into office promising many democratic reforms but ended up ruling the country for thirty-four years as an absolute dictator. In the process of modernization, the human toll was high, class distinctions were polarized, and Mexico was changed forever.

Event 12: The Battle of Isandlwana: 1879

1. An Army Surgeon's Account of the Battle of Isandlwana

Early in the Zulu war, on the vast plain of Isandlwana, twenty thousand Zulu warriors wiped out most of the main British invasion column and attacked a British army hospital.

FOREWORD

I n 1543 a Polish astronomer named Nicolaus Copernicus published a book entitled *De revolutionibus orbium coelestium* in which he theorized that Earth revolved around the Sun. In 1688, during the Glorious Revolution, Dutch prince William of Orange invaded England and overthrew King James II. In 1922 Irish author James Joyce's novel *Ulysses*, which describes one day in Dublin, was published.

Although these events are seemingly unrelated, occurring in different nations and in different centuries, they all share the distinction of having changed the world. Although Copernicus's book had a relatively minor impact at the time of its publication, it eventually had a momentous influence. The Copernican system provided a foundation on which future scientists could develop an accurate understanding of the solar system. Perhaps more importantly, it required humanity to contemplate the possibility that Earth, far from occupying a special place at the center of creation, was merely one planet in a vast universe. In doing so, it forced a reevaluation of the Christian cosmology that had served as the foundation of Western culture. As professor Thomas S. Kuhn writes, "The drama of Christian life and the morality that had been made dependent upon it would not readily adapt to a universe in which the earth was just one of a number of planets."

Like the Copernican revolution, the Glorious Revolution of 1688–1689 had a profound influence on the future of Western societies. By deposing James II, William and his wife, Mary, ended the Stuart dynasty, a series of monarchs who had favored the Catholic Church and had limited the power of Parliament for decades. Under William and Mary, Parliament passed the Bill of Rights, which established the legislative supremacy of Parliament and barred Roman Catholics from the throne. These actions initiated the gradual process by which the power of the government of England shifted from the monarchy to Parliament, establishing a democratic system that would be copied, with some variations, by the United States and other democratic societies worldwide.

Whereas the Glorious Revolution had a major impact in the political sphere, the publication of Joyce's novel *Ulysses* represented a revolution in literature. In an effort to capture the sense of chaos and discontinuity that permeated the culture in the wake of World War I, Joyce did away with the use of straightforward narrative that had dominated fiction up to that time. The novel, whose structure mirrors that of Homer's *Odyssey*, combines realistic descriptions of events with passages that convey the characters' inner experience by means of a technique known as stream of consciousness, in which the characters' thoughts and feelings are presented without regard to logic or narrative order. Due to its departure from the traditional modes of fiction, *Ulysses* is often described as one of the seminal works of modernist literature. As stated by Pennsylvania State University professor Michael H. Begnal, "*Ulysses* is the novel that changed the direction of 20th-century fiction written in English."

Copernicus's theory of a sun-centered solar system, the Glorious Revolution, and James Joyce's *Ulysses* are just three examples of time-bound events that have had far-reaching effects— for better or worse—on the progress of human societies worldwide. History is made up of an inexhaustible list of such events. In the twentieth century alone, for example, one can isolate any number of world-shattering moments: the first performance of Igor Stravinsky's ballet *The Rites of Spring* in 1913; Japan's attack on Pearl Harbor on December 7, 1941; the launch of the satellite *Sputnik* on October 4, 1957. These events variously influenced the culture, society, and political configuration of the twentieth century.

Greenhaven Press's Events That Changed the World series is designed to help readers learn about world history by examining seemingly random events that have had the greatest influence on the development of cultures, societies, and governments throughout the ages. The series is divided into sets of several anthologies, with each set covering a period of one hundred years. Each volume begins with an introduction that provides essential context on the time period being covered. Then, the major events of the era are covered by means of primary and secondary sources. Primary sources include firsthand accounts, speeches, correspondence, and other materials that bring history alive. Secondary sources analyze the profound effects the events had on the world. Each reading is preceded by an introduction that puts it in context and emphasizes the event's importance in the ongoing evolution of world history. Additional features add to the value of the series: An annotated table of contents and an index allow readers to quickly locate material of interest. A chronology provides an easy reference for contextual information. And a bibliography offers opportunities for further exploration. All of these features help to make the Events That Changed the World series a valuable resource for readers interested in the major events that have shaped the course of humanity.

INTRODUCTION

To understand the marked changes that occurred during the decades of the 1860s through the 1880s, it is interesting to consider a few contrasts. In 1865 news of Abraham Lincoln's assassination took months to reach California and England the same way news of Caesar's defeat of the Gauls traveled in 52 B.C.—by sailing ship, horseback, and word of mouth. In 1887, when Queen Victoria celebrated her Golden Jubilee, she used the recently devised telegraph to send a message that reached Australia, Canada, India, and central Africa within a couple of hours. A person who underwent surgery in 1860 was offered no more pain relief than was available to patients in ancient Egypt. By 1880 anesthetics completely blocked patients' perception of pain even during major surgical procedures. Thus, much of the way we live today has its roots in the discoveries and inventions of the late nineteenth century, a period of rapid technological advances and rapid shifts in social and cultural values.

Reforms in education, for example, had both immediate and far-reaching effects. Before 1860 most schools in Europe and America were privately funded and operated by local churches or convents. A series of educational reforms in the United States, England, Austria, Hungary, Italy, Switzerland, the Netherlands, and Belgium led to the establishment of the first secular, state-funded public education systems. As access to education increased, the percentage of American children enrolled in school rose from 35 percent in 1830 to more than 70 percent in 1880. Literacy rates soared accordingly. Historians estimate that in 1860 only about 60 percent of the U.S. population could read and write. By 1880 the literacy rate was over 80 percent and rising steadily. Educational reform had similar success throughout the developed world; by the end of the nineteenth century, for example, the literacy rate in Japan approached 90 percent.

A literate, educated public naturally demanded more and more varied reading material. By 1880 scientific and technological advances in photographic and printing processes allowed for greater production and distribution of published material including books, magazines, and newspapers. Mass-produced publications became a primary communications tool, leading to a better-informed and more politically active middle class.

In 1850 a magazine's or newspaper's average readership was approximately twenty-five thousand. By 1890 average circulation had increased to well over half a million. It was the beginning of the mass-media revolution. By the turn of the century, magazine and newspaper subscriptions would exceed 1 million in the United States and 2 million in Europe. Circulation of the French daily *Le Petit Journal* was 2 million in 1900, and London's illustrated *Daily Mirror* had a 1-million-copy print run by 1910. The number of mass-circulation periodicals markedly increased as well. In 1865 seven hundred periodicals were published in the United States. By 1885 the total number of published periodicals had increased to more than thirty-three hundred.

Reading was not the only pastime that boomed in the 1860s and 1870s. Population growth and migration dramatically increased the size of cities in Europe and the United States, and the concentration of people along with an economic upsurge sparked the growth of all kinds of popular entertainment. In London, ten major theaters were constructed between 1875 and 1895. Eleven large theatrical venues opened in Germany during the same period, and music halls and cabarets flourished in European capitals. Covent Garden, a London concert hall, was expanded to seat four thousand. The Paris Opera, a seventeen-story structure more than 118,000 square feet in size, capable of seating two thousand people, opened with great fanfare in 1875. Public sporting arenas were built to accommodate rising interest in mass-spectator professional sports such as English football. At venues from sporting events to music halls, affordably priced tickets offered rich and poor alike the opportunity to enjoy a wide variety of entertainment.

Revolutions in Scientific and Political Theory

One of the most dramatic and far-reaching scientific developments of the era came in the study of biology. In 1859 English naturalist Charles Darwin published his seminal work, *On the Origin of Species,* outlining the theory of evolution. The book's publication was highly anticipated; all 1,250 copies of the first edition sold out on the first day of its release. By 1860 the book was in wide distribution and attracting both devoted followers and harsh criticism. Darwin explained the origination of species in terms of a struggle for existence, in which only the "fittest" organisms survive. As a young researcher in the isolated Galá-pagos Islands, Darwin had observed unique plants and animals that led him to conclude that species adapt to their specific, changing environment through a series of subtle physical changes that are passed on to offspring. Individuals that do not acquire needed physical characteristics eventually die out; individuals that do survive become more varied, gradually giving rise to new species, a process Darwin called natural selection.

Darwin's book was the first published work to present scientifically sound, well-supported evidence for evolution. His theory challenged long-standing and deeply held scientific and religious beliefs about the creation of the world, man's place in nature, and, some argued, even the existence of God. Along with his 1871 work, *The Descent of Man,* it inspired intense scientific and intellectual inquiry, formed the basis of new branches of science such as genetics and ecology, and sparked wider interest in anthropology and archaeology.

Another written work of this era proved to have equally far-reaching effects in a different sphere, politics. In 1867 German political philosopher Karl Marx published the first volume of his great study of the economics of capitalism, *Das Kapital.* Marx argued that the course of history is determined by economic factors. He predicted the inevitable collapse of capitalism, which he blamed for materialism, social inequity, class struggle, and the inevitable rise of world communism through working-class revolt. Marx attempted to prove his theory mathematically, with elaborate equations that many found incomprehensible, but though his formulas faded, his ideas took hold. Marx's work is widely regarded as the principal inspiration of modern political radicalism, the Socialist movement, and the Communist revolutions of the twentieth century. His philosophy led not only to violent political upheaval and (contrary to his predictions) no less brutally repressive political regimes, but also to progressive reforms such as social security, income tax legislation, public health programs, and laws protecting the rights and fair wages of laborers.

Technology Revolutionizes Daily Life

The scientific, medical, and technological breakthroughs of the 1860s and 1870s were important factors in all of these broad political and intellectual shifts, but their effects on everyday life were every bit as revolutionary. In the United States, raw materials and manpower that had been diverted to Civil War industries were redirected after 1865 to mass production of consumer goods. Industrialization meant abundance and affordability, and increased production capacity created a need for new things to produce. Suddenly, ordinary people could buy durable and inexpensive shoes, clothing, appliances, and household furnishings.

It is hard to measure the radical effect of Thomas Edison's invention of the incandescent lightbulb in 1879 because, as Donna Yankowitz writes on the history Web site *Turn of the Century,* "Once a house or business had electricity installed for lighting an almost endless amount of other items could be developed and sold: electric irons, fans, electric motors, [and] refrigerators." Electrification was soon followed by the development of indoor plumbing and running water, which transformed the routines of housework and hygiene. The development of rapid transportation—primarily, the railroad—during this era was invaluable in commercial and territorial expansion, but this too had equally important small-scale benefits. Ordinary people simply could get from one place to another more quickly and more conveniently than ever before.

Events That Changed the World: 1860–1880 helps readers understand not only the practical applications and immediate effects of discovery and invention, and the dizzying effects of rapid change on social and cultural institutions, but also the ways the key events of this period shaped the modern world.

Alexander II Frees the Serfs to Modernize Russia

by Nicholas V. Riasanovsky

The Edict of Emancipation was the means by which Russian czar Alexander II freed the Russian serfs. Emancipation of the serfs was the first in a series of many reforms that transformed Russia into a modern nation. Numbering more than one-third of the total population of Russia, the serfs were peasants who were indentured to their masters and had no personal freedom or civil rights. They were allowed to live on the land in exchange for working it. They were tied to laboring on farms and never received any formal education or opportunities to advance themselves. For many generations, the serfs lived in abject poverty and had little means to improve their condition.

Prior to modernization, the Russian economy was rural, feudal, and tied to the indentured labor provided by the serfs. It was a complicated system, but it needed to be changed in order for Russia to modernize and compete in the expanding international economy. Some serfs were owned by wealthy royalty, and others were owned by simple farmers who were nearly as poor as the serfs who worked their land. Other serfs were under direct control of the government. Because of these diverse kinds of relationships between serfs and landowners, many considerations had to be taken into account when drafting the provisions that allowed for fair transfer of ownership and land. Alexander II was committed to making this change and began the process during the first year of his rule in 1855. Although some resisted, the human rights of the serfs became an important issue as well as the desperate need to modernize and improve the Russian economy. Alexander II assembled a council of the finest minds from the areas of law, academia, and economics and assigned them the task of drafting provisions for the emancipation of the serfs.

There is no question that at midcentury Russia was in dire straits. Many domestic problems in Russia had been ignored for centuries, and the condition of the serfs was a glaring example. The abolition of serfdom signified the establishment of capitalism as the dominant socioeconomic form in Russia. The following essay describes how the serfs came to be freed, the process by which this momentous change came to pass, and the modern reforms it inspired.

Nicholas V. Riasanovsky is a professor emeritus of Russian and European history at the University of California, Berkeley, where he has taught since 1957. He has also published many books, including *The Image of Peter the Great in Russian History and Thought* and *The Emergence of Romanticism.*

A lexander II succeeded his father, Nicholas I, on the Russian throne at the age of thirty-seven. He had received a rather good education as well as considerable practical training in the affairs of state. Alexander's teachers included the famous poet [Vasily] Zhukovsky, who has often been credited with developing humane sentiments in his pupil. To be sure, Grand Duke Alexander remained an obedient son of his strong-willed father and showed no liberal inclinations prior to becoming emperor. Indeed he retained an essentially conservative mentality and attitude throughout his life. Nor can Alexander II be considered a strong or a talented man. Yet, forced by the logic of the situation, the new monarch decided to undertake, and actually carried through, fundamental reforms unparalleled in scope in Russian history since Peter the Great. These reforms, although extremely important, failed to cure all the ills of Russia and in fact led to new problems and perturbations, which resulted, among other things, in the assassination of the "Tsar-Liberator."

The last words of Alexander II's manifesto announcing the end of the Crimean War promised reform, and this produced a strong impression on the public. The new emperor's first measures, enacted even before the termination of hostilities, included the repeal of some of the Draconian restrictions of Nicholas I's final years, such as those on travel abroad and on the number of students attending universities. All this represented a promising prologue; the key issue, as it was for Alexander I, the last ruler who wanted to transform Russia, remained serfdom. However, much had changed in regard to serfdom during the intervening, fifty or fifty-five years. Human bondage . . . satisfied less and less effectively the economic needs of the Russian Empire. With the growth of a money economy and competition for markets, the deficiencies of low-grade serf labor became ever more obvious. Many landlords, especially those with small holdings, could barely feed their serfs; and the gentry accumulated an enormous debt. As we know, free labor, whether really free or merely the contractual labor of someone else's serfs, became more common throughout the Russian economy during the first half of the nineteenth century. Moreover, the serfs perhaps declined in absolute number in the course of that period, while their numerical weight in relation to other classes certainly declined: from 58 per cent of the total population of Russia in 1811 to 44.5 per cent on the eve of the "great reforms.". . . In any event, whether the landlords were willing to recognize it or not—and large vested interests seldom obey even economic reason—serfdom was becoming increasingly anachronistic.

Other powerful arguments for emancipation reinforced the economic. Oppressed and exasperated beyond endurance, the serfs kept rising against their masters. While no nineteenth-century peasant insurrection could at all rival the [Yemelyan Ivanovich] Pugachev rebellion [1773–1774 Russian peasant uprising], the uprisings became more frequent and on the whole more serious. [Russian historian] Semevsky, using official records, had counted 550 peasant uprisings in the nineteenth century prior to the emancipation. A Soviet historian, Ignatovich, raised the number to 1,467 and gave the following breakdown: 281 peasant rebellions, that is, 19 per cent of the total, in the period from 1801 to 1825; 712 rebellions, 49 per cent, from 1826 to 1854; and 474 uprisings, or 32 per cent, in the six years and two months of Alexander II's reign before the abolition of serfdom. Ignatovich emphasized that the uprisings also increased in length, in bitterness, in the human and material losses involved,

and in the military effort necessary to restore order. Still more recently, Okun and other Soviet scholars have further expanded Ignatovich's list of uprisings. Moreover, Soviet scholarship claims
that peasant rebellions played the decisive role in the emancipation of the serfs, and that on the eve of the "great reforms" Russia experienced in effect a revolutionary situation. Although exaggerated, this view cannot be entirely dismissed. Interestingly,
it was the Third Department [police force], the gendarmery, that
had stressed the danger of serfdom during the reign of Nicholas I.
Besides rising in rebellion, serfs ran away from their masters,
sometimes by the hundreds and even by the thousands. On occasion large military detachments had to be sent to intercept
them. Pathetic mass flights of peasants, for example, would follow rumors that freedom could be obtained somewhere in the
Caucasus [geographical area between the Black and Caspian
seas], while crowds of serfs tried to join the army during the
Crimean War, because they mistakenly believed that they could
thereby gain their liberty.

Moral Grounds for Emancipation

A growing sentiment for emancipation, based on moral grounds,
also contributed to the abolition of serfdom. The Decembrists, the
Slavophiles, the Westernizers, the Petrashevtsy, some supporters
of Official Nationality, together with other thinking Russians, all
wanted the abolition of serfdom. As education developed in Russia, and especially as Russian literature came into its own, humane feelings and attitudes became more widespread. Such leading writers as [Aleksandr] Pushkin and particularly [Ivan]
Turgenev, who in 1852 published in book form his magnificent
collection of stories, *Sportsman's Sketches*, where serfs were depicted as full-blown, and indeed unforgettable, human beings, no
doubt exercised an influence. In fact, on the eve of the abolition
of serfdom in Russia—in contrast to the situation with slavery in
the American South—virtually no one defended that institution;
the arguments of its proponents were usually limited to pointing
out the dangers implicit in such a radical change as emancipation.

Finally, the Crimean War provided additional evidence of the
deficiencies and dangers of serfdom which found reflection both
in the poor physical condition and listlessness of the recruits and
in the general economic and technological backwardness of the
country. Besides, . . . Russia had essentially to rely on a standing

army without a reserve, because the government was afraid to allow soldiers to return to villages.

At the time of the coronation, about a year after his assumption of power, Alexander II, addressing the gentry of Moscow, made the celebrated statement that it would be better to begin to abolish serfdom from above than to wait until it would begin to abolish itself from below, and asked the gentry to consider the matter. Although the government experienced great difficulty in eliciting any initiative from the landlords on the subject of emancipation, it finally managed to seize upon an offer by the gentry of the three Lithuanian provinces to discuss emancipation without land. The ensuing imperial rescript made it clear that emancipation was indeed official policy and, furthermore, that emancipation would have to be with land. At about the same time restrictions were lifted from the discussion of the abolition of serfdom in the press. In the wave of expectation and enthusiasm that swept the liberals and radicals after the publication of the rescript even [Russian writer and political agitator Aleksandr] Herzen exclaimed to Alexander II: "Thou hast conquered, O Galilean!"

Writing the Edict

Eventually, in 1858, gentry committees were established in all provinces to consider emancipation, while a bureaucratic Main Committee of nine members was set up in St. Petersburg. Except for a few diehards, the landlords assumed a realistic position and accepted the abolition of serfdom once the government had made its will clear, but they wanted the reform to be carried out as advantageously for themselves as possible. The gentry of southern and south-central Russia, with its valuable, fertile soil, wanted to retain as much land as possible and preferred land to a monetary recompense; the gentry of northern and north-central Russia, by contrast, considered serf labor and the resulting obrok as their main asset and, therefore, while relatively willing to part with much of their land, insisted on a high monetary payment in return for the loss of serf labor. Gentry committees also differed on such important issues as the desirable legal position of the liberated serfs and the administration to be provided for them.

The opinions of provincial committees went to the Editing Commission—actually two commissions that sat together and formed a single body—created at the beginning of 1859 and composed of public figures interested in the peasant question, such as the Slavophiles George Samarin and Prince Vladimir Cherkassky, as well as of high officials. After twenty months of work the Editing Commission submitted its plan of reform to the Main Committee, whence it went eventually to the State Council. After its quick consideration by the State Council, Alexander II signed the emancipation manifesto on March 3, 1861—February 19, Old Style. Public announcement followed twelve days later.

Throughout its protracted and cumbersome formulation and passage the emancipation reform faced the hostility of conservatives in government and society. That a far-reaching law was finally enacted can be largely credited to the determined efforts of so-called "liberals," including officials such as Nicholas Miliutin, the immediate assistant to the minister of the interior and the leading figure in the Editing Commission, and participants from the public like George Samarin. Two members of the imperial family, the tsar's brother Grand Duke Constantine and the tsar's aunt Grand Duchess Helen, belonged to the "liberals." More important, Alexander II himself repeatedly sided with them, while his will became law for such devoted bureaucrats as Jacob Rostovtsev—a key figure in the emancipation—who cannot be easily classified as either "conservative" or "liberal." The emperor in effect forced the speedy passage of the measure through an antagonistic State Council, which managed to add only one noxious provision to the law, that permitting a "pauper's allotment," which will be mentioned later. Whereas the conservatives defended the interests and rights of the gentry, the "liberals" were motivated by their belief that the interests of the state demanded a thoroughgoing reform and by their views of what would constitute a just settlement.

The law of the nineteenth of February abolished serfdom. Thenceforth human bondage was to disappear from Russian life. It should be noted, however, that, even if we exclude from consideration certain temporary provisions that prolonged various serf obligations for different periods of time, the reform failed to give the peasants a status equal to that of other social classes: they had to pay a head tax, were tied to their communes, and were judged on the basis of customary law. In addition to landowners' serfs, the new freedom was extended to peasants on the lands of the imperial family and to the huge and complex category of state peasants.

Together with their liberty, serfs who had been engaged in farming received land: household serfs did not. While the detailed provisions of the land settlement were extremely complicated and different from area to area, the peasants were to obtain roughly half the land, that part which they had been tilling for themselves, the other half staying with the landlords. They had to repay the landlords for the land they acquired and, because few serfs could pay anything, the government compensated the gentry owners by means of treasury bonds. Former serfs in turn were to reimburse the state through redemption payments spread over a period of forty-nine years. As an alternative, serfs could take one-quarter of their normal parcel of land, the so-called "pauper's allotment," and pay nothing. Except in the Ukraine and a few other areas, land was given not to individual peasants, but to a peasant commune—called an *obshching* or *mir*, the latter term emphasizing the communal gathering of peasants to settle their affairs—which divided the land among its members and was responsible for taxes, the provision of recruits, and other obligations to the state.

Not the Best Circumstances

The emancipation of the serfs can be called a great reform, although an American historian probably exaggerated when he proclaimed it to be the greatest legislative act in history. It directly affected the status of some fifty-two million peasants, over twenty million of them serfs of private land owners. That should be compared, for example, with the almost simultaneous liberation of four million black slaves in the United States, obtained as a result of a huge Civil War, not by means of a peaceful legal process. The moral value of the emancipation was no doubt tremendous, if incalculable. It might be added that the arguments of [Mikhail] Pokrovsky and some other historians attempting to show that the reform was a clever conspiracy between the landlords and the government at the expense of the peasants lack substance: they are contradicted both by the actual preparation and passage of the emancipation legislation and by its results, for it contributed in a major manner to the decline of the gentry. By contrast, those Soviet specialists and others who emphasize the importance of the abolition of serfdom for the development of capitalism in Russia stand on much firmer ground. The specific provisions of the new settlement have also been defended and even praised, especially on the basis of the understanding that the arrangement had to be a compromise, not a confiscation of everything the gentry owned. Thus, the emancipation of serfs in Russia has been favorably compared to that in Prussia at the beginning of the nineteenth century, and land allotments of Russian peasants, to allotments in several other countries.

And yet the emancipation reform also deserves thorough criticism. The land allotted to the former serfs turned out to be insufficient. While in theory they were to retain the acreage that they had been tilling for themselves prior to 1861, in fact they received 18 per cent less land. Moreover, in the fertile southern provinces their loss exceeded the national average, amounting in some cases to 40 per cent or more of the total. Also, in the course of the partitioning, former serfs often failed to obtain forested areas or access to a river with the result that they had to assume additional obligations toward their onetime landlords to satisfy their needs. . . . Other scholars have stressed the overpopulation and underemployment among former serfs who, at least after a period of transition, were no longer obliged to work for the landlord and at the same time had less land to cultivate for themselves. State peasants, although by no means prosperous, received, on the whole, better terms than did the serfs of private owners.

The financial arrangement proved unrealistic and impossible to execute. Although liberated serfs kept meeting as best they could the heavy redemption payments, which were not related to their current income, the arrears kept mounting. By the time the redemption payments were finally abolished in 1905, former serfs paid, counting the interest, one and one half billion rubles for the land initially valued at less than a billion. It should be noted that while officially the serfs were to redeem only the land, not their persons, actually the payments included a concealed recompense for the loss of serf labor. Thus, more had to be paid for the first unit of land, the first desiatina, than for the following units. As a whole the landlords of southern Russia received 340 million rubles for land valued at 280 million; those of northern Russia, where obrok prevailed, 340 million rubles for land worth 180 million rubles. The suspect Polish and Polonized landlords of the western provinces constituted an exception, for they were given slightly less money than the just price of their land.

The transfer of land in most areas to peasant communes rather than to individual peasants probably represented another major error, although this is an extremely complex issue. Arguments in favor of the commune ranged from the Slavophile admiration of the moral aspects of that institution to the desire on the part of the government to have taxes and recruits guaranteed by means of communal responsibility and to the assertion that newly liberated peasants would not be able to maintain themselves but could find protection in the commune. While some of these and other similar claims had a certain validity—indeed, as a practical matter the government could hardly have been expected to break up the commune at the same time the serfs were being freed—the disadvantages of the commune outweighed its advantages. Of most importance was the fact that the commune tended to perpetuate backwardness, stagnation, and overpopulation in the countryside precisely when Russian agriculture drastically needed improvement and modernization.

The emancipation reform disappointed Russian radicals, who considered it inadequate, and it also, apparently, failed to satisfy the peasantry, or at least many peasants, for a rash of agrarian disturbances followed the abolition of serfdom, and the misery, despair, and anger in the countryside remained a powerful threat to imperial Russia until the very end of imperial rule.

Other "Great Reforms"

The emancipation of the serfs made other fundamental changes much more feasible. Alexander II and his assistants turned next to the reform of local government, to the establishment of the so-called zemstvo system. For centuries local government had remained a particularly weak aspect of Russian administration and life. The arrangement that the "Tsar-Liberator" inherited dated from Catherine the Great's legislation and combined bureaucratic management with some participation by the local gentry; the considerable manorial jurisdiction of the landlords on their estates formed another prominent characteristic of the pre-reform countryside. The new law, enacted in January 1864, represented a strong modernization and democratization of local government, as well as a far-reaching effort on the part of the state to meet the many pressing needs of rural Russia and to do this largely by stimulating local initiative and activity. Institutions of self-government, zemstvo assemblies and boards, were created at both the district and provincial levels—the word zemstvo itself connotes land, country, or people, as distinct from the central government. The electorate of the district zemstvo assemblies consisted of three categories: the towns, the peasant communes, and all individual landowners, including those not from the gentry. Representation was proportional to landownership, with some allowance for the possession of real estate in towns. The elections were indirect. Members of district assemblies, in turn, elected from their own midst, regardless of class, delegates to their provincial assembly. Whereas the district and provincial zemstvo assemblies, in which the zemstvo authority resided, met only once a year to deal with such items as the annual budget and basic policies, they elected zemstvo boards to serve continuously as the executive agencies of the system and to employ professional staffs. A variety of local needs fell under the purview of zemstvo institutions: education, medicine, veterinary service, insurance, roads, the establishment of food reserves for emergency, and many others. . . .

In 1870 a municipal reform reorganized town government and applied to towns many of the principles and practices of the zemstvo administration. The new town government, which was "to take care of and administer urban economy and welfare," consisted of a town council and a town administrative board elected by the town council. The town council was elected by all property owners or taxpayers; but the election was according to a three-class system, which gave the small group on top that paid a third of the total taxes a third of the total number of delegates, the middle tax payers another third, and the mass at the bottom that accounted for the last third of taxes the remaining third of delegates.

A New Legal System

At the end of 1864, the year that saw the beginning of the zemstvo administration, another major change was enacted into law: the reform of the legal system. The Russian judiciary needed reform probably even more than the local government did. Archaic, bureaucratic, cumbersome, corrupt, based on the class system rather than on the principle of equality before the law, and relying entirely on a written and secret procedure, the old system was thoroughly hated by informed and thinking Russians. . . . Radicals attached special importance to a reform of the judiciary. A conservative, the Slavophile Ivan Aksakov, reminisced: "The old court! At the mere recollection of it one's hair stands on end and one's flesh begins to creep!" The legislation of 1864 fortunately marked a decisive break with that part of the Russian past.

The most significant single aspect of the reform was the separation of the courts from the administration. Instead of constituting merely a part of the bureaucracy, the judiciary became an independent branch of government. Judges were not to be dismissed or transferred, except by court action. Judicial procedure acquired a largely public and oral character instead of the former bureaucratic secrecy. The contending parties were to present their cases in court and have adequate legal support. In fact, the reform virtually created the class of lawyers in Russia, who began rapidly to acquire great public prominence. Two legal procedures, the general and the abbreviated one, replaced the chaos of twenty-one alternate ways to conduct a case. Trial by jury was introduced for serious criminal offenses, while justices of the peace were established to deal with minor civil and criminal cases. The courts were organized into a single unified system with the Senate at the apex. All Russians were to be equal before the law and receive the same treatment. Exceptions to the general system were the military and ecclesiastical courts, together with special courts for peasants who lived for the most part by customary law.

The reform of the judiciary, which was largely the work of the Minister of Justice Dmitrii Zamiatnin, his extremely important assistant Serge Zarudny, and several other enlightened officials, proved to be the most successful of the "great reforms." Almost overnight it transformed the Russian judiciary from one of the worst to one of the best in the civilized world. Later the government tried on occasion to influence judges for political reasons; and, what is more important, in its struggle against radicalism and revolution it began to withdraw whole categories of legal cases from the normal procedure of 1864 and to subject them to various forms of the courts-martial. But, while the reform of the judiciary could be restricted in application, it could not be undone by the imperial government; and, as far as the reform extended, modern justice replaced arbitrariness and confusion. Russian legal reform followed Western, especially French, models, but . . . these models were skillfully adapted to Russian needs. It might be added that the courts, as well as the zemstvo institutions, acquired political significance, for they served as centers of public interest and enjoyed a somewhat greater freedom of expression than was generally allowed in Russia.

A New Military

A reorganization of the military service in 1874 and certain changes within the army have usually been grouped as the last "great reform." Inspired by military needs and technically complex, the reform nevertheless exercised an important general impact on Russian society and contributed to the modernization and democratization of the country. It was executed by Minister of War Dmitrii Miliutin, Nicholas Miliutin's brother, who wanted to profit by the example of the victorious Prussian army. He introduced a variety of significant innovations, of which the most important was the change in military service. The obligation to serve was extended from the lower classes alone to all Russians, while at the same time the length of active service was drastically reduced—from twenty-five years in the beginning of Alexander II's reign to six after the reform of 1874—and a military reserve was organized. Recruits were to be called up by lot; different exemptions were provided for hardship cases; and, in addition, terms of enlistment were shortened for those with education, a not unwarranted provision in Russian conditions. Miliutin also reformed military law and legal procedure, abolished corporal punishment in the army, strove to improve the professional quality of the officer corps and to make it somewhat more democratic, established specialized military schools, and, a particularly important point, introduced elementary education for all draftees. Measures similar to Miliutin's were carried out in the navy by Grand Duke Constantine.

Other reforms under Alexander II included such financial innovations as Valery Tatarinov's establishment of a single state treasury, publication of the annual budget, and the creation in 1866 of the State Bank to centralize credit and finance, as well as generally liberalizing steps with regard to education and censorship.

The "great reforms" went a long way toward transforming Russia. To be sure, the empire of the tsars remained an autocracy, but it changed in many other respects. Vastly important in themselves, the government's reforms also helped to bring about sweeping economic and social change. . . . The growth of capitalism in Russia, the evolution of the peasantry, the decline of the gentry, the rise of the middle class, particularly the professional group, and also of the proletariat—all were affected by Alexander II's legislation. Indeed, Russia began to take long strides on the road to becoming a modern nation. Nor could the changes be undone: there was no return to serfdom or to pre-reform justice.

The Difficult Sixties

However, although the government could not return to the old ways, it could stop advancing on the new road and try to restrict and limit the effectiveness of the changes. And in fact it attempted to do so in the second half of Alexander II's reign, under Alexander III, and under Nicholas II until the Revolution of 1905. While the need for reforms had been apparent, the rationale of reaction proved less obvious and more complicated. For one thing, the reforms, as we know, had their determined opponents in official circles and among the Russian gentry, who did their best to reverse state policy. Special circumstances played their part, such as peasant uprisings, student disturbances, the unexplained fires of 1862, the Polish rebellion of 1863, and Dmitrii Karakozov's attempt to assassinate the emperor in 1866. More important was the fact that the government failed to resolve the fundamental dilemma of change: where to stop. The "great reforms," together with the general development of Russia and the intellectual climate of the time, led to pressure for further reform. Possibly the granting of a constitutional monarchy and certain other concessions would have satisfied most of the demand and provided stability for the empire. But neither Alexander II nor certainly his successors were willing to go that far. Instead they turned against the proponents of more change and fought to preserve the established order. The "great reforms" had come only after the Crimean War had demonstrated the total bankruptcy of the old system, and they owed little to any far-reaching liberalism or vision on the part of Alexander II and his immediate associates. The sequel showed how difficult it was for the imperial government to learn new ways.

The Edict of Emancipation

by Alexander II

The following document is the edict of emancipation that legalized freedom of the Russian serfs. It outlines the provisions and means by which personal serfdom would be abolished and the guidelines for the transfer of land from landlords to peasants. This involved what was known as redemption payments, through which the peasants could work the land and purchase it from the landlords in a series of forty-nine annual sums. Until redemption began, the law allowed for a period of "temporary obligation" during which time the peasants held the land but paid for it in money or labor. Some serfs choose to accept "beggarly allotments"—one-fourth of the prescribed amount of land without any monetary obligations. In many cases, the initial stage before redemption dragged on for more than twenty years, and many serfs ended up paying more for the land than it was actually worth.

Alexander II was born in 1818 and became czar in 1855 upon the death of his father, Nicholas I. Influenced by Russia's defeat in the Crimean War (1853–1856) and by peasant unrest, Alexander embarked on a modernization and reform program. The most important reform was the emancipation of the serfs. This led to many more reforms that ultimately transformed Russia into a modern nation and, ironically, set the stage for the populist movement in the late 1860s and eventually the Russian Revolution. Radical activities increased sharply because many people believed that Alexander's reforms were far too moderate. The government arrested and prosecuted hundreds of student demonstrators and activists, and a terror-

Alexander II, "Edict of Emancipation," March 3, 1861.

ist backlash resulted. Also, many peasants who were discontented with their provisions became active in protests against the government. After several attempts on his life, Alexander II was assassinated by a hand-thrown terrorist's bomb on March 13, 1881, and was succeeded by his son, Alexander III.

By the Grace of God We, Alexander II, Emperor and Autocrat of All Russia, King of Poland, Grand Duke of Finland, and so forth, make known to all Our faithful subjects:

Called by Divine Providence and by the sacred right of inheritance to the throne of Our Russian ancestors, We vowed in Our heart to fulfill the mission which is entrusted to Us and to surround with Our affection and Our Imperial solicitude all Our faithful subjects of every rank and condition, from the soldier who nobly defends the country to the humble artisan who works in industry; from the career official of the state to the ploughman who tills the soil.

Examining the condition of classes and professions comprising the state, We became convinced that the present state legislation favours the upper and middle classes, defines their obligations, rights, and privileges, but does not equally favour the serfs, so designated because in part from old laws and in part from custom they have been hereditarily subjected to the authority of landowners, who in turn were obligated to provide for their well-being. Rights of nobles have been hitherto very broad and legally ill defined, because they stem from tradition, custom, and the good will of the noblemen. In most cases this has led to the establishment of good patriarchal relations based on the sincere, just concern and benevolence on the part of the nobles, and on affectionate submission on the part of the peasants. Because of the decline of the simplicity of morals, because of an increase in the diversity of relations, because of the weakening of the direct paternal attitude of nobles toward the peasants, and because noble rights fell sometimes into the hands of people exclusively concerned with their personal interests, good relations weakened. The way was opened for arbitrariness burdensome for the peasants and detrimental to their welfare, causing them to be indifferent to the improvement of their own existence.

These facts had already attracted the attention of Our predecessors of glorious memory, and they had adopted measures aimed at improving the conditions of the peasants; but these measures were ineffective, partly because they depended on the free, generous action of nobles, and partly because they affected only some localities, by virtue of special circumstances or as an experiment. Thus Alexander I issued a decree on free farmers, and the late Imperial Russian Emperor Nicholas, Our beloved father, promulgated one dealing with the serfs. In the Western guberniias, inventory regulations determine the peasant land allotments and their obligations. But decrees on free farmers and serfs have been carried out on a limited scale only.

We thus became convinced that the problem of improving the condition of serfs was a sacred inheritance bequeathed to Us by Our predecessors, a mission which, in the course of events, Divine Providence has called upon Us to fulfill.

We have begun this task by expressing Our confidence in the Russian nobility, which has proved on so many occasions its devotion to the Throne, and its readiness to make sacrifices for the welfare of the country.

We have left to the nobles themselves, in accordance with their own wishes, the task of preparing proposals for the new organization of peasant life, proposals that would limit their rights over the peasants, and the realization of which would inflict on them some material losses. Our confidence was justified. Through members of the guberniia committees, who had the trust of the nobles' gatherings, the nobility voluntarily renounced its right to own serfs. These committees, after collecting the necessary data, have formulated proposals on a new arrangement for serfs and their relationship with the nobles.

The Arrangements Are Finalized

These proposals were diverse, because of the nature of the problem. They have been compared, collated, systematized, rectified, and finalized in the Main Committee instituted for that purpose; and these new arrangements dealing with the peasants and domestics of the nobility have been examined in the State Council.

Having invoked Divine assistance, We have resolved to execute this task.

On the basis of the above-mentioned new arrangements, the serfs will receive in time the full rights of free rural inhabitants.

The nobles, while retaining their property rights on all the lands belonging to them, grant the peasants perpetual use of their domicile in return for a specified obligation; and, to assure their livelihood as well as to guarantee fulfillment of their obligations toward the government, grant them a portion of arable land fixed by the said arrangements, as well as other property.

While enjoying these land allotments, the peasants are obliged, in return, to fulfill obligations to the noblemen fixed by the same arrangements. In this condition, which is temporary, the peasants are temporarily obligated.

At the same time, they are granted the right to purchase their domicile, and, with the consent of the nobles, they may acquire in full ownership the arable lands and other properties which are allotted them for permanent use. Following such acquisition of full ownership of land, the peasants will be freed from their obligations to the nobles for the land thus purchased and will become free peasant landowners.

A special decree dealing with domestics will establish a temporary status for them, adapted to their occupations and their needs. At the end of two years from the day of the promulgation of this decree, they shall receive full freedom and some temporary immunities.

In accordance with the fundamental principles of these arrangements, the future organization of peasants and domestics will be determined, the order of general peasant administration will be established, and the rights given to the peasants and to the domestics will be spelled out in detail, as will the obligations imposed on them toward the government and the nobles.

A Complex Transition

Although these arrangements, general as well as local, and the special supplementary rules affecting some particular localities, estates of petty nobles, and peasants working in factories and enterprises of the nobles, have been as far as possible adapted to economic necessities and local customs; nevertheless, to preserve the existing order where it presents reciprocal advantages, we leave it to the nobles to reach a friendly understanding with the peasants and to reach agreements on the extent of the land allotment and the obligations stemming from it, observing, at the same time, the established rules to guarantee the inviolability of such agreements.

This new arrangement, because of its complexity, cannot be put into effect immediately; a time of not less than two years is necessary. During this period, to avoid all misunderstanding and to protect public and private interests, the order actually existing on the estates of nobles should be maintained until the new order shall become effective.

Towards that end, We have deemed it advisable:

1. To establish in each guberniia a special Office of Peasant Affairs, which will be entrusted with the affairs of the peasant land communes established on the estates of the nobility.

2. To appoint in every uezd [district] justices of the peace to solve all misunderstandings and disputes which may arise from the new arrangement, and to organize from these justices district assemblies.

3. To organize Peace Offices on the estates of the nobles, leaving the peasant land communes as they are, and to open volost offices in the large villages and unite small peasant land communes under one volost office.

4. To formulate, verify, and confirm in each village commune or estate a charter which would enumerate, on the basis of local conditions, the amount of land allotted to the peasants for permanent use, and the scope of their obligations to the nobleman for the land as well as for other advantages which are granted.

5. To put these charters into practice as they are gradually approved on each estate, and to put them into effect everywhere within two years from the date of publication of this manifesto.

6. Until that time, peasants and domestics must be obedient towards their nobles, and scrupulously fulfill their former obligations.

7. The nobles will continue to keep order on their estates, with the right of jurisdiction and of police, until the organization of volosts and of volost courts.

Aware of the unavoidable difficulties of this reform, We place Our confidence above all in the graciousness of Divine Providence, which watches over Russia.

We also rely upon the zealous devotion of Our nobility, to whom We express Our gratitude and that of the entire country as well, for the unselfish support it has given to the realization of Our designs. Russia will not forget that the nobility, motivated by its respect for the dignity of man and its Christian love of its neighbour, has voluntarily renounced serfdom, and has laid the foundation of a new economic future for the peasants. We also expect that it will continue to express further concern for the realization of the new arrangement in a spirit of peace and benevolence, and that each nobleman will realize, on his estate, the great civic act of the entire group by organizing the lives of his peasants and his domestics on mutually advantageous terms, thereby setting for the rural population a good example of a punctual and conscientious execution of state regulations.

The examples of the generous concern of the nobles for the welfare of peasants, and the gratitude of the latter for that concern give Us the hope that a mutual understanding will solve most of the difficulties, which in some cases will be inevitable during the application of general rules to the diverse conditions on some estates, and that thereby the transition from the old order to the new will be facilitated, and that in the future mutual confidence will be strengthened, and a good understanding and a unanimous tendency towards the general good, will evolve.

To facilitate the realization of these agreements between the nobles and the peasants, by which the latter may acquire in full ownership their domicile and their land, the government will lend assistance, under special regulations, by means of loans or transfer of debts encumbering an estate.

Common Sense Should Not Waver

We rely upon the common sense of Our people. When the government advanced the idea of abolishing serfdom, there developed a partial misunderstanding among the unprepared peasants. Some were concerned about freedom and unconcerned about obligations. But, generally, the common sense of the country has not wavered, because it has realized that every individual who enjoys freely the benefits of society owes it in return certain positive obligations; according to Christian law every individual is subject to higher authority (*Romans*, chap. xiii, 1); everyone must fulfill his obligations, and, above all, pay tribute, dues, respect, and honour (Ibid. chap. xi, 7). What legally belongs to nobles cannot be taken away from them without adequate compensation, or through their voluntary concession; it would be contrary to all justice to use the land of the nobles without assuming responsibility for it.

And now We confidently expect that the freed serfs, on the eve of a new future which is opening to them, will appreciate and recognize the considerable sacrifices which the nobility has made on their behalf.

Social Responsibility Is Essential

They should understand that by acquiring property and greater freedom to dispose of their possessions, they have an obligation to society and to themselves to live up to the letter of the new law by a loyal and judicious use of the rights which are now granted to them. However beneficial a law may be, it cannot make people happy if they do not themselves organize their happiness under protection of the law. Abundance is acquired only through hard work, wise use of strength and resources, strict economy, and above all, through an honest God-fearing life.

The authorities who prepared the new way of life for the peasants and who will be responsible for its inauguration will have to see that this task is accomplished with calmness and regularity, taking the timing into account in order not to divert the attention of cultivators away from their agricultural work. Let them zealously work the soil and harvest its fruits so that they will have a full granary of seeds to return to the soil which will be theirs.

And now, Orthodox people, make the sign of the cross, and join with Us to invoke God's blessing upon your free labour, the sure pledge of your personal well-being and the public prosperity.

Given at St. Petersburg, March 3, the year of Grace 1861, and the seventh of Our reign. Alexander.

The Beginning of the End of the American Civil War

by James M. McPherson

The Battle of Antietam changed the entire course of the American
Civil War (1861–1865). Antietam was Confederate general Robert
E. Lee's first invasion of the North and led to President Abraham
Lincoln's issuance of the Emancipation Proclamation. Not only was
Antietam the first major Civil War engagement on Northern soil, it
was also the bloodiest single day in American history. The battle
claimed more than twenty-three thousand men killed, wounded, and
missing, more than the total deaths in all previous American wars
combined. Antietam not only halted Lee's bold invasion of the
North, but it also provided President Lincoln with the victory he
needed to announce the abolition of slavery in the South. Five days
later, the Emancipation Proclamation was issued.

The Civil War had a marked effect in Europe, where it strained
the economy as well as diplomatic relations with Great Britain and
France. With the proclamation of emancipation, President Lincoln
was able to broaden the base of the war and may have prevented
England and France from ultimately lending support to the South.

The following essay describes the lasting and profound repercussions of the Battle of Antietam and the issuance of the Emancipa-

James M. McPherson, *Crossroads of Freedom: Antietam*. New York: Oxford University Press,
2002. Copyright © 2002 by James M. McPherson. All rights reserved. Reproduced by permission of Oxford University Press, Inc.

tion Proclamation in both America and in Europe. Although Lee's
Confederate army was not decisively defeated at Antietam, his
grand strategy was. Northern morale increased dramatically, and
Confederate military momentum was checked.

James M. McPherson is the author of more than twelve books on
the Civil War and countless articles, review, and essays. He received
a PhD from Johns Hopkins University in 1963 and has taught at
Princeton University for more than thirty-five years. His comprehensive history of the American Civil War, *Battle Cry of Freedom*,
won the Pulitzer Prize for History in 1989.

On September 13 President [Abraham] Lincoln had taken
an hour out of his crisis schedule to meet with a dele-
gation of Chicago clergymen bearing a petition urging
a proclamation of emancipation. Lincoln did not tell them that a
draft of such a proclamation had rested in a desk drawer for almost two months while he waited for the military situation to improve. That situation had instead gotten worse—and never more
so than at that moment when [Robert E.] Lee was in Maryland,
[Union commander George] McClellan had not confronted him
yet, panic reigned in much of the North, and the war seemed on
the verge of being lost. Lincoln's private secretary John Hay recalled this period as one of "fearful anxiety" and "almost unen-
durable tension" for the president.

Some of that tension spilled over into his remarks to the dele-
gation, which had claimed that emancipation was the will of
God. "If it is probable that God would reveal his will to others,
on a point so connected with my duty," said Lincoln testily, "it
might be supposed he would reveal it directly to me." In present
circumstances, with Rebel armies in Maryland and Kentucky and
threatening Pennsylvania and Ohio, "what *good* would a proclamation of emancipation from me do . . . when I cannot even enforce the Constitution in the rebel States? . . . I don't want to issue a document the whole world will see must necessarily be
inoperative, like the Pope's bull against the comet!"

Divine Intervention

A week later all had changed. Five days after Antietam Lincoln
called a special meeting of the Cabinet. He reminded members
of their decision two months earlier to postpone issuance of an

emancipation proclamation. "I think the time has come now," the president continued. "I wish it was a better time. . . . The action of the army against the rebels has not been quite what I should have best liked. But they have been driven out of Maryland." When the enemy was at Frederick, Lincoln had made a "promise to myself and (hesitating a little) to my Maker" that "if God gave us the victory in the approaching battle, [I] would consider it an indication of Divine will" in favor of emancipation. Perhaps recalling his conversation with the Chicago clergymen, Lincoln suggested that Antietam was God's sign that "he had decided this question in favor of the slaves." Therefore, said the president, he intended that day to issue the proclamation warning Confederate states that unless they returned to the Union by January 1, 1863, their slaves "shall be then, thenceforward, and forever free."

A Shattering Consequence

Perhaps no consequence of Antietam was more momentous than this one. It changed the character of the war, as General-in-Chief [Henry] Halleck noted in a communication to Ulysses S. Grant: "There is now no possible hope of reconciliation. . . . We must conquer the rebels or be conquered by them. . . . Every slave withdrawn from the enemy is the equivalent of a white man put *hors de combat.*" The proclamation would apply only to states in rebellion, which produced some confusion because it thus seemed to "liberate" those slaves who were mostly beyond Union authority while leaving in bondage those in the border states. This apparent anomaly caused disappointment among some abolitionists and radical Republicans. But most of them recognized that the commander in chief's legal powers extended only to *enemy* property. Some of that "property," however, *would* be freed by the Proclamation or by the practical forces of war because thousands of contrabands in Confederate states were already within Union lines.

And in any event, the symbolic power of the Proclamation changed the war from one to restore the Union into one to destroy the old Union and build a new one purged of human bondage. "GOD BLESS ABRAHAM LINCOLN!" blazoned Horace Greeley's *New York Tribune* on September 23. "It is the beginning of the end of the rebellion; the beginning of the new life of the nation." The Emancipation Proclamation "is one of those stupendous facts in human history which marks not only an era in the

progress of the nation, but an epoch in the history of the world."
Speaking for African Americans, Frederick Douglass declared:
"We shout for joy that we live to record this righteous decree."

Democrats almost unanimously denounced the Proclamation
and vowed to campaign against it in the fall congressional elections. Many border-state Unionists also complained loudly. Lincoln had already discounted this opposition, which had once concerned him so greatly. He had tried in vain to get the border states
to move voluntarily, but now "we must make the forward movement" without them, he told the Cabinet. "They [will] acquiesce,
if not immediately, soon." As for the Democrats, "their clubs
would be used against us take what course we might."

The Army Is Divided

More serious, perhaps, was the potential for opposition in the
army, especially by McClellanite officers in the Army of the
Potomac. There was good reason for worry about this. General
Fitz-John Porter branded Lincoln's document "the absurd proclamation of a political coward." It has "caused disgust, and ex-
pressions of disloyalty, to the views of the administration" in the
army, wrote Porter privately. McClellan himself considered the
Proclamation "infamous" and told his wife that he could not
"make up my mind to fight for such an accursed doctrine as that
of a servile insurrection." McClellan consulted Democratic
friends in New York, who advised him "to submit to the Presdt's
proclamation & quietly continue doing my duty as a soldier." He
even took action to quiet loose talk among some of his subordinates about marching on Washington to overthrow the government. On October 7 McClellan issued a general order reminding
the army of its duty of obedience to civil authority. "The remedy
for political errors, if any are committed," he noted in a none-too-
subtle reference to the forthcoming elections, "is to be found in
the action of the people at the polls."

The issue of emancipation would continue—at times danger-
ously—to divide the army and the Northern public for another
six months or more. But in the end, as the *Springfield* (Mass.)
Republican predicted on September 24, 1862, it would "be sus-
tained by the great mass of the loyal people." These were the
people who agreed with Lincoln's words in his message to Congress on December 1, 1862: "Without slavery the rebellion could
never have existed; without slavery it could not continue." The

Springfield Republican proved to be right when it anticipated that "by the courage and prudence of the President, the greatest social and political revolution of the age will be triumphantly carried through in the midst of a civil war."

A Signal Impact Abroad

The battle of Antietam and the Emancipation Proclamation had a signal impact abroad. Only two days before the first news of Antietam arrived in London, the Earl of Shaftesbury, Prime Minister Palmerston's son-in-law, told Confederate envoys John Slidell and James Mason that "the event you so strongly desire," a British-French offer of mediation and diplomatic recognition, "is very close at hand." But the news of Union victories in Maryland came as "a bitter draught and a stunning blow" to friends of the Confederacy in Britain, wrote the secretary of the American legation. "They express as much chagrin as if they themselves had been defeated."

The London *Times* certainly was stunned by the "exceedingly remarkable" outcome of Antietam. "An army demoralized by a succession of failures," in the words of a *Times* editorial, "has suddenly proved at least equal, and we may probably say superior, to an army elated with triumph and bent upon a continuation of its conquests." Calling Lee's invasion of Maryland "a failure," the normally pro-Southern *Times* admitted that "the Confederates have suffered their first important check exactly at the period when they might have been thought most assured of victory." Other British newspapers expressed similar sentiments. South Mountain and Antietam restored "our drooping credit here," reported American Minister Charles Francis Adams. Most Englishmen had expected the Confederates to capture Washington, and "the surprise" at their retreat "has been quite in proportion. . . . As a consequence, less and less appears to be thought of mediation and intervention."

Europe Balks at Intervention

Adams's prognosis was correct. Prime Minister Palmerston now backed away from the idea of intervention. The only favorable condition for mediation "would be the great success of the South against the North," he pointed out to Foreign Secretary [John] Russell on October 2. "That state of things seemed ten days ago to be approaching," but with Antietam "its advance has been lately checked." Thus "the whole matter is full of difficulty," and nothing could be done until the situation became more clear. By October 22 it *was* clear to Palmerston that Confederate defeats had ended any chance for successful mediation. "I am therefore inclined to change the opinion I wrote you when the Confederates seemed to be carrying all before them, and I am [convinced] . . . that we must continue merely to be lookers-on till the war shall have taken a more decided turn."

Russell and [British chancellor of the exchequer William] Gladstone, plus Napoleon of France, did not give up easily. The French asked Britain to join in a proposal for a six-month's armistice in the American war during which the blockade would be lifted, cotton exports would be renewed, and peace negotiations would begin. France also approached Russia, which refused to take part in such an obviously pro-Confederate scheme. On November 12 the British Cabinet also rejected it after two days of discussions in which Secretary for War Sir George Cornewall Lewis led the opposition to intervention. In a letter six days later to King Leopold of Belgium, who favored the Confederacy and supported intervention, Palmerston explained the reasons for Britain's refusal to act. "Some months ago" when "the Confed-

The Battle of Antietam, depicted above, was the single bloodiest day in American history.

erates were gaining ground to the North of Washington, and events seemed to be in their favor," an "opportunity for making some communication" appeared imminent. But "the tide of war changed its course and the opportunity did not arrive."

Dashed Hopes for Confederate Support

Most disappointed of all by this outcome was James Mason, who was left cooling his heels by the British refusal to recognize his own diplomatic status as well as that of his government. On the eve of the arrival in London of news about Antietam, Mason had been "much cheered and elated" by initial reports of Lee's invasion. "Recognition is not far off," he had written on October 1st. Dashed hopes soured Mason on the "obdurate" British, and he felt "that I should terminate the mission here." He decided to stay on, but never again did his mission come so close to success as in September 1862.

The preliminary Emancipation Proclamation further eroded the Confederacy's chances for diplomatic recognition—though at first it seemed to have the contrary effect. The American minister to France warned [Union secretary of state William H.] Seward to expect the "most mischievous efforts" by Confederate sympathizers "to pervert and misconstrue the motives which have prompted the proclamation." Anti-American conservatives in Britain and France, and even some liberals, professed to see the Proclamation not as a genuine antislavery act but as a cynical attempt to deflect European opinion or as a desperate effort to encourage a slave insurrection. If Lincoln really wanted to free the slaves, they asked, why did he announce that the Proclamation would apply to states where he had no power and exempt those where he did? The Proclamation was "cold, vindictive, and entirely political," wrote the British chargé d'affaires in Washington. Lord Russell, who had earlier censured the Lincoln administration for *not* acting against slavery, now perversely pronounced the preliminary Proclamation a vile encouragement to "acts of plunder, of incendiarism, and of revenge."

The Anti-American Press

The "incitement to insurrection" theme was based on a phrase in Lincoln's preliminary Proclamation stating that the government "will do no act or acts to repress" slaves "in any acts they may make for their actual freedom." Lincoln, of course, meant that the army would not return slaves coming into Union lines. But the anti-American press (which included most major newspapers in Britain) seized upon this phrase as an excuse to berate Lincoln and the Union cause.

The *London Times* was the most notorious in this regard, seeing it as an opportunity to reopen the issue of British intervention on humanitarian grounds. With this Proclamation, declared the *Times*, Lincoln "will appeal to the black blood of the African; he will whisper of the pleasures of spoil and of the gratification of yet fiercer instincts; and when the blood begins to flow and shrieks come piercing through the darkness, Mr. LINCOLN will wait till the rising flames tell that all is consummated, and then he will rub his hands and think that revenge is sweet." Many other British newspapers took their cue from the *Times*, branding the Proclamation "the last resort of a bewildered statesman," "the wretched makeshift of a pettifogging lawyer," "the last arm of vengeance . . . to carry the war of the knife to private homes where women and children are left undefended."

British friends of the Union understood this "demoniacal cry" by "the ghouls of the English press" for what it was. "In England," wrote John Stuart Mill to an American friend, "the proclamation has only increased the venom of those who after taunting you for so long with caring nothing for abolition, now reproach you for your abolitionism as the worst of your crimes." But these "wretched effusions," said Mill, came from conservatives "who so hate your democratic institutions that they would be sure to inveigh against you whatever you did, and are enraged at no longer being able to taunt you with being false to your own principles." Benjamin Moran, the acidulous secretary of the American legation, wrote that the response of the British press to the Proclamation exposed "the hollowness of the anti-slavery professions of these people. . . . Altho' they know that Mr. Lincoln is in earnest, they so desire us to be crushed that they won't believe him."

The Majority Speaks

But the "effusions" of the anti-American press probably did not reflect the sentiments of a majority of the British people. And this majority was not silent. The *London Morning Star* spoke for them when it pronounced the Proclamation "a gigantic stride in the paths of Christian and civilized progress—the turning point in the history of the American commonwealth—an act only second in courage and probable results to the Declaration of Independence." In November 1862, pro-Union forces in Britain began to organize meetings and circulate petitions in favor of the Proclamation. When Lincoln on January 1st confounded European cynics who had predicted that he would never issue the final Proclamation, pro-Union sentiments in Britain grew stronger. Lincoln implicitly responded to criticisms of the preliminary Proclamation by stating in the final version that emancipation was "an act of justice" as well as a military measure, and by enjoining freed slaves to refrain from violence.

Even though the final Proclamation exempted states or parts of states containing one-quarter of all slaves, it nevertheless announced a new war aim that foreshadowed universal emancipation if the North won the war. A black Methodist clergyman in Washington, Henry M. Turner, rejoiced that "the time has come in the history of this nation, when the downtrodden and abject black man can assert his rights, and feel his manhood. . . . The first day of January, 1863, is destined to form one of the most memorable epochs in the history of the world."

International Appeal

As recognition of this truth dawned across the Atlantic, huge mass meetings in Britain adopted pro-Union resolutions and sent copies to the American legation—some fifty of them in all. "The Emancipation Proclamation has done more for us here than all our former victories and all our diplomacy," wrote Henry Adams from London on January 23. "It is creating an almost convulsive reaction in our favor all over this country." The largest of the meetings, at Exeter Hall in London, "has had a powerful effect on our newspapers and politicians," wrote Richard Cobden, one of the foremost pro-Union members of Parliament. "It has closed the mouths of those who have been advocating the side of the South. Recognition of the South, by England, whilst it bases itself on Negro slavery, is an impossibility." Similar reports came from elsewhere in Europe. "The anti-slavery position of the government is at length giving us a substantial foothold in European circles," wrote the American minister to the Netherlands. "Everyone can understand the significance of a war where emancipation is written on one banner and slavery on the other.". . .

Lincoln had shelved his proposed edict of emancipation to wait for a victory that might never come. But it did, along the ridges and in the woods and cornfields between Antietam Creek and the Potomac River in the single bloodiest day in all of American history.

The victory at Antietam could have been more decisive. The same was true of two lesser victories that followed at Corinth and Perryville. But Union armies had stymied the supreme Confederate efforts. Foreign powers backed away from intervention and recognition, and never again came so close to considering them. Lincoln issued his Emancipation Proclamation. Northern voters chastised but did not overthrow the Republican party, which forged ahead with its program to preserve the Union and give it a new birth of freedom. Here indeed was a pivotal moment.

Momentous Consequences

No other campaign and battle in the war had such momentous, multiple consequences as Antietam. In July 1863 the dual Union triumphs at Gettysburg and Vicksburg struck another blow that blunted a renewed Confederate offensive in the East and cut off the western third of the Confederacy from the rest. In September 1864 [Confederate general William Tecumseh] Sherman's capture of Atlanta reversed another decline in Northern morale and set the stage for the final drive to Union victory. These also were pivotal moments. But they would never have happened if the triple Confederate offensives in Mississippi, Kentucky, and most of all Maryland had not been defeated in the fall of 1862.

Contemporaries recognized Antietam as the preeminent turning point of the war. Jefferson Davis was depressed by the outcome there because the Confederacy had put forth its maximum effort and failed. Two of the war's best corps commanders, who fought each other at Antietam (and several other battlefields), Winfield Scott Hancock for the Union and James Longstreet for the Confederacy, made the same point. In 1865 Hancock looked back on the past four years and concluded that "the battle of Antietam was the heaviest disappointment the rebels had met with. They then felt certain of success and felt that they should carry the war so far into the Northern states that the recognition of the Confederacy would have been a necessity." And twenty years after the war, Longstreet wrote simply: "At Sharpsburg was sprung the keystone of the arch upon which the Confederate cause rested." Only with the collapse of that arch could the future of the United States as one nation, indivisible and free, be assured.

Emancipation of the Slaves Will Have Far-Reaching Effects

by Frederick Douglass

Abraham Lincoln initially entered the Civil War with the singular goal of preserving the Union. Although slavery was the singular, unresolvable issue, Lincoln did not think Union soldiers would fight to free the slaves. Quite early on, however, it became clear that an end to slavery was the key to victory. Such a shift in popular opinion did not come about by accident. The men and women of the antislavery movement worked persistently to educate the public to this fact, and Frederick Douglass was its most outspoken and effective leader. Douglass recognized the revolutionary implications of the Civil War and clearly saw it as an opportunity to put an end to slavery and set an example for the rest of the world.

The most famous African American opponent of slavery, Douglass won world fame when his first autobiography, *The Narrative of the Life of Frederick Douglass, an American Slave*, was published in 1845. A newspaper editor, a talented speaker, and the author of countless essays, editorials, articles, and books, Frederick Douglass's career spanned nearly the entire nineteenth century and touched on issues of race and gender that resonate more than a century beyond his death in 1895.

Frederick Douglass, "Emancipation Proclaimed," *Douglass' Monthly*, October 1862.

The following article is from the October 1862 issue of Frederick Douglass's newspaper, *Douglass' Monthly*. The article was published immediately following President Abraham Lincoln's September 22 announcement of the Emancipation Proclamation. Douglass discusses the significance of this event both at home and abroad and how he believes that the single act of emancipation will allow the Union to prevail. He also writes that the act of emancipation will secure the place of a free and honorable America in the international community, where America will, higher than ever, "sit as a queen among the nations of the earth."

Common sense, the necessities of the war, to say nothing of the dictation of justice and humanity have at last prevailed. We shout for joy that we live to record this righteous decree. *Abraham Lincoln*, President of the United States, Commander-in-Chief of the army and navy, in his own peculiar, cautious, forbearing and hesitating way, slow, but we hope sure, has, while the loyal heart was near breaking with despair, proclaimed and declared: *"That on the First of January, in the Year of Our Lord One Thousand, Eight Hundred and Sixty-three, All Persons Held as Slaves Within Any State or Any Designated Part of a State, The People Whereof Shall Then be in Rebellion Against the United States, Shall be Thenceforward and Forever Free."* "Free forever" oh! long enslaved millions, whose cries have so vexed the air and sky, suffer on a few more days in sorrow, the hour of your deliverance draws nigh! Oh! Ye millions of free and loyal men who have earnestly sought to free your bleeding country from the dreadful ravages of revolution and anarchy, lift up now your voices with joy and thanksgiving for with freedom to the slave will come peace and safety to your country. President Lincoln has embraced in this proclamation the law of Congress passed more than six months ago, prohibiting the employment of any part of the army and naval forces of the United States, to return fugitive slaves to their masters, commanded all officers of the army and navy to respect and obey its provisions. He has still further declared his intention to urge upon the Legislature of all the slave States not in rebellion the immediate or gradual abolishment of slavery. But read the proclamation for it is the most important of any to which the President of the United States has ever signed his name.

Opinions will widely differ as to the practical effect of this measure upon the war. All that class at the North who have not lost their affection for slavery will regard the measure as the very worst that could be devised, and as likely to lead to endless mischief. All their plans for the future have been projected with a view to a reconstruction of the American Government upon the basis of compromise between slaveholding and non-slaveholding States. The thought of a country unified in sentiments, objects and ideas, has not entered into their political calculations, and hence this newly declared policy of the Government, which contemplates one glorious homogeneous people, doing away at a blow with the whole class of compromisers and corrupters, will meet their stern opposition. Will that opposition prevail? Will it lead the President to reconsider and retract? Not a word of it. Abraham Lincoln may be slow, Abraham Lincoln may desire peace even at the price of leaving our terrible national sore untouched, to fester on for generations, but Abraham Lincoln is not the man to reconsider, retract and contradict words and purposes solemnly proclaimed over his official signature.

No Turning Back

The careful, and we think, the slothful deliberation which he has observed in reaching this obvious policy, is a guarantee against retraction. But even if the temper and spirit of the President himself were other than what they are, events greater than the President, events which have slowly wrung this proclamation from him may be relied on to carry him forward in the same direction. To look back now would only load him with heavier evils, while diminishing his ability, for overcoming those with which he now has to contend. To recall his proclamation would only increase rebel pride, rebel sense of power and would be hailed as a direct admission of weakness on the part of the Federal Government, while it would cause heaviness of heart and depression of national enthusiasm all over the loyal North and West. No, Abraham Lincoln will take no step backward. His word has gone out over the country and the world, giving joy and gladness to the friends of freedom and progress wherever those words are read, and he will stand by them, and carry them out to the letter. If he has taught us to confide in nothing else, he has taught us to confide in his word. The want of Constitutional power, the want of military power, the tendency of the measure to intensify Southern hate, and to exasperate the rebels, the tendency to drive from him all that class of Democrats at the North, whose loyalty has been conditioned on his restoring the union as it was, slavery and all, have all been considered, and he has taken his ground notwithstanding. The President doubtless saw, as we see, that it is not more absurd to talk about restoring the union, without hurting slavery, than restoring the union without hurting the rebels. As to exasperating the South, there can be no more in the cup than the cup will hold, and that was full already. The whole situation having been carefully scanned, before Mr. Lincoln could be made to budge an inch, he will now stand his ground. Border State influence, and the influence of half-loyal men, have been exerted and have done their worst. The end of these two influences is implied in this proclamation. Hereafter, the inspiration as well as the men and the money for carrying on the war will come from the North, and not from half-loyal border states.

Repercussions in Europe and at Home

The effect of this paper upon the disposition of Europe will be great and increasing. It changes the character of the war in European eyes and gives it an important principle as an object, instead of national pride and interest. It recognizes and declares the real nature of the contest, and places the North on the side of justice and civilization, and the rebels on the side of robbery and barbarism. It will disarm all purpose on the part of European Government to intervene in favor of the rebels and thus cast off at a blow one source of rebel power. All through the war thus far, the rebel ambassadors in foreign countries have been able to silence all expression of sympathy with the North as to slavery. With much more than a show of truth, they said that the Federal Government, no more than the Confederate Government, contemplated the abolition of slavery.

But will not this measure be frowned upon by our officers and men in the field? We have heard of many thousands who have resolved that they will throw up their commissions and lay down their arms, just so soon as they are required to carry on a war against slavery. Making all allowances for exaggeration there are doubtless far too many of this sort in the loyal army. Putting this kind of loyalty and patriotism to the test, will be one of the best collateral effects of the measure. Any man who leaves the field on such a ground will be an argument in favor of the proclamation, and will prove that his heart has been more with slavery than with his country. Let the army be cleansed from all such pro-slavery vermin, and its health and strength will be greatly improved. But there can be no reason to fear the loss of many officers or men by resignation or desertion. We have no doubt that the measure was brought to the attention of most of our leading Generals, and blind as some of them have seemed to be in the earlier part of the war, most of them have seen enough to convince them that there can be no end to this war that does not end slavery. At any rate, we may hope that for every pro-slavery man that shall start from the ranks of our loyal army, there will be two anti-slavery men to fill up the vacancy, and in this war one truly devoted to the cause of Emancipation is worth two of the opposite sort.

President Abraham Lincoln and Union general George B. McClellan meet at Antietam, where Lincoln delivered the Emancipation Proclamation on September 22, 1862.

Conditions for Abolition

Whether slavery will be abolished in the manner now proposed by President Lincoln, depends of course upon two conditions, the first specified and the second implied. The first is that the slave States shall be in rebellion on and after the first day of January 1863 and the second is we must have the ability to put down that rebellion. About the first there can be very little doubt. The South is thoroughly in earnest and confident. It has staked everything upon the rebellion. Its experience thus far in the field has rather increased its hopes of final success than diminished them. Its armies now hold us at bay at all points, and the war is confined to the border States slave and free. If Richmond were in our hands and Virginia at our mercy, the vast regions beyond would still remain to be subdued. But the rebels confront us on the Potomac, the Ohio, and the Mississippi. Kentucky, Maryland, Missouri, and Virginia are in debate on the battlefields and their people are divided by the line which separates treason from loyalty. In short we are yet, after eighteen months of war, confined to the outer margin of the rebellion. We have scarcely more than touched the surface of the terrible evil. It has been raising large quantities of food during the past summer. While the masters have been fighting abroad, the slaves have been busy working at home to supply them with the means of continuing the struggle. They will not down at the bidding of this Proclamation, but may be safely relied upon till January and long after January. A month or two will put an end to general fighting for the winter. When the leaves fall we shall hear again of bad roads, winter quarters and spring campaigns. The South which has thus far withstood our arms will not fall at once before our pens. All fears for the abolition of slavery arising from this apprehension may be dismissed. Whoever, therefore, lives to see the first day of next January, should Abraham Lincoln be then alive and President of the United States, may confidently look in the morning papers for the final proclamation, granting freedom, and freedom forever, to all slaves within the rebel States. On the next point nothing need be said. We have full power to put down the rebellion. Unless one man is more than a match for four, unless the South breeds braver and better men than the North, unless slavery is more precious than liberty, unless a just cause kindles a feebler enthusiasm than a wicked and villainous one, the men of the loyal States will put down this rebellion and slavery, and all the sooner will they put down that rebellion by coupling slavery with that object. Tenderness towards slavery has been the loyal weakness during the war. Fighting the slaveholders with one hand and holding the slaves with the other, has been fairly tried and has failed. We have now inaugurated a wiser and better policy, a policy which is better for the loyal cause than an hundred thousand armed men. The Star Spangled Banner is now the harbinger of Liberty and the millions in bondage, inured to hardships, accustomed to toil, ready to suffer, ready to fight, to dare and to die, will rally under that banner wherever they see it gloriously unfolded to the breeze. Now let the Government go forward in its mission of Liberty as the only condition of peace and union, by weeding out the army and navy of all such officers as the late Col. Miles, whose sympathies are now known to have been with the rebels. Let only the men who assent heartily to the wisdom and the justice of the anti-slavery policy of the Government be lifted into command; let the black man have an arm as well as a heart in this war, and the tide of battle which has thus far only waved backward and forward, will steadily set in our favor. The rebellion suppressed, slavery abolished, and America will, higher than ever, sit as a queen among the nations of the earth.

The Road Ahead

Now for the work. During the interval between now and next January, let every friend of the long enslaved bondman do his utmost in swelling the tide of anti-slavery sentiment, by writing, speaking, money and example. Let our aim be to make the North a unit in favor of the President's policy, and see to it that our voices and votes, shall forever extinguish that latent and malignant sentiment at the North, which has from the first cheered on the rebels in their atrocious crimes against the union, and has systematically sought to paralyze the national arm in striking down the slaveholding rebellion. We are ready for this service or any other, in this, we trust the last struggle with the monster slavery.

The First Labor Union Changes the World
Economy: 1864

Address and Provisional Rules of the International Working Men's Association

by Karl Marx

Although short-lived and plagued with internal strife and financial crisis, the establishment of the International Working Men's Association in London marked the beginning of a new kind of trade unionism whose influences are widely established today all over the world. The association was inaugurated by Karl Marx at a meeting in St. Martin's Hall in London on September 28, 1864.

The European economic crisis of 1857 and the political crisis of 1859 culminated in the Franco-Austrian War in 1860 (the War of Italian Independence), and all over Europe there ensued a general awakening of the bourgeoisie and of the proletariat alike. In Great Britain there was the additional influence of the American Civil War (1861–1864), for this led to a crisis in the cotton trade, which left British textile workers in terrible distress. This economic crisis, which began toward the close of the 1850s, led to an epidemic of

Karl Marx, *Address and Provisional Rules of the International Working Men's Association.* London: Labour & Socialist International, 1924.

strikes and renewed labor movements all over Europe. The resulting "trades councils" and labor leaders integrated the local movements and promoted the international organization of the proletariat.

It was inevitable that in 1864 an international labor association would form. Involved in the organization from early on, Karl Marx, then living in London, was elected to the association's provisional general council. He became the dominant figure in the organization, drafting its general rules and a carefully worded inaugural address that was designed to safeguard unity of purpose. The goal of the First International was to unite all workers for the purpose of achieving political power along the lines set down by Marx and Friedrich Engels in *The Communist Manifesto* (1848). Marx viewed the association as a vehicle for revolution, but others viewed it as a means to anarchy. Power struggles within the organization greatly weakened it, and the clash between Marx and the anarchist Mikhail Bakunin led to its complete disintegration in 1876.

Karl Marx is best known for giving socialism and the labor movement of our day a scientific foundation. He was born in Trier (Rhenish Prussia) in 1818 and died in London in 1883. Best known for his landmark works *Das Kapital* and *The Communist Manifesto* (penned with collaborator Friedrich Engels), Marx wrote countless essays, letters, and articles in his lifetime and was dedicated to the emancipation of the working classes. The following is Marx's inaugural address of the International Working Men's Association.

I t is a great fact that the misery of the working masses has not diminished from 1848 to 1864, and yet this period is unrivalled for the development of its industry and the growth of its commerce. In 1850, a moderate organ of the British middle-class, of more than average information, predicted that if the exports and imports of England were to rise 50 per cent., English pauperism would sink to zero. Alas! on April 7th, 1864, the Chancellor of the Exchequer [William Gladstone] delighted his Parliamentary audience by the statement that the total import and export trade of England had grown in 1863 "to £443,955,000, that astonishing sum about three times the trade of the comparatively recent epoch of 1843." With all that he was eloquent upon "poverty." "Think," he exclaimed, "of those who are on the border of that region," upon "wages . . . not increased;" upon "hu-

man life . . . in nine cases out of ten but a struggle of existence."
He did not speak of the people of Ireland, gradually replaced by
machinery in the North, and by sheep-walks in the south, though
even the sheep in that unhappy country are decreasing it is true
not at so rapid a rate as the men. He did not repeat what then had
been just betrayed by the highest representatives of the upper ten
thousand in a sudden fit of terror. When the garotte [street rob-
bery] panic had reached a certain height, the House of Lords
caused an inquiry to be made into, and a report to be published
upon, transportation and penal servitude. Out came the murder
in the bulky Blue Book of 1863, and proved it was, by official
facts and figures, that the worst of the convicted criminals, the
penal serfs of England and Scotland, toiled much less and fared
far better than the agricultural labourers of England and Scotland. But this was not all. When, consequent upon the civil war
in America, the operatives of Lancashire and Cheshire were
thrown upon the streets, the same House of Lords sent to the
manufacturing districts a physician commissioned to investigate
into the smallest possible amount of carbon and nitrogen, to be
administered in the cheapest and plainest form, which, on an average, might just suffice to "avert starvation diseases." Dr. Smith,
the medical deputy, ascertained that 28,000 grains of carbon and
1,330 grains of nitrogen were the weekly allowance that would
keep an average adult . . . just over the level of starvation diseases, and he found furthermore that quantity pretty nearly to
agree with the scanty nourishment to which the pressure of extreme distress had actually reduced the cotton operatives. But
now mark! The same learned Doctor was later on again deputed
by the medical officer of the Privy Council to inquire into the
nourishment of the poorer labouring classes. The results of his
researches are embodied in the "Sixth Report on Public Health,"
published by order of Parliament in the course of the present
year. What did the Doctor discover? That the silk weavers, the
needle women, the kid glovers, the stocking weavers, and so
forth, received, on an average, not even the distressed pittance of
the cotton operatives, not even the amount of carbon and nitrogen "just sufficient to avert starvation diseases."

The Uneven Distribution of Wealth

"Moreover," we quote from the report, "as regards the examined
families of the agricultural population, it appeared that more

than a fifth were with less than the estimated sufficiency of carbonaceous food: that more than one third were with less than the estimated sufficiency of nitrogenous food, and that in three counties (Berkshire, Oxfordshire and Somersetshire,) insufficiency of nitrogenous food was the average local diet." "It must be remembered," adds the official report, "that privation of food is very reluctantly borne, and that, as a rule, great poorness of diet will only come when other privations have preceded it. . . . Even cleanliness will have been found costly or difficult, and if there still be self-respectful endeavours to maintain it, every such endeavour will represent additional pangs of hunger. These are painful reflections, especially when it is remembered that the poverty to which they advert is not the deserved poverty of idleness: in all cases it is the poverty of working populations. Indeed, the work which obtains the scanty pittance of food is, for the most part, excessively prolonged." The report brings out the strange and rather unexpected fact, "That of the divisions of the United Kingdom," England, Wales, Scotland, and Ireland, "the agricultural population of England," the richest division, "is considerably the worst fed," but that even the agricultural labourers of Berkshire, Oxfordshire, and Somersetshire, fare better than great numbers of skilled indoor operatives of the East of London.

Karl Marx

Such are the official statements published by order of Parliament in 1864, during the millennium of free trade, at a time when the Chancellor of the Exchequer told the House of Commons that "the average condition of the British labourer has improved in a degree we know to be extraordinary and unexampled in the history of any country or any age." Upon these official congratulations jars the dry remark of the official Public Health Report: "The public health of a country means the health of its masses, and the masses will scarcely be healthy unless, to their very base, they be at least moderately prosperous."

Dazzled by the "Progress of the Nation," statistics dancing before his eyes, the Chancellor of the Exchequer exclaims in wild ecstacy: "From 1642 to 1852 the taxable income of the country increased by six per cent.; in the eight years from 1853 to 1861, it has increased from the basis taken in 1853, 20 per cent., the fact is so astonishing as to be almost incredible. . . . This intoxicating augmentation of wealth and power," adds Mr. Gladstone, "is entirely confined to classes of property."

The Broken Health of the Workers

If you want to know under what conditions of broken health, tainted morals, and mental ruin, that "intoxicating augmentation of wealth and power entirely confined to classes of property" was, and is being produced by the classes of labour, look to the picture hung up in the last "Public Health Report" of the workshops of tailors, printers and dressmakers. Compare the "Report of the Children's Employment Commission" of 1863, where it is stated, for instance, that—"The potters as a class, both men and women, represent a much degenerated population, both physically and mentally," that the unhealthy child is an unhealthy parent in his turn," that a progresssive determination of the race must go on and that "the degenerescence of the population of Staffordshire would be even greater were it not for the constant recruiting from the adjacent country, and the intermarriages with more healthy races.". . . And who has not shuddered at the paradoxical statement made by the inspectors of factories, and illustrated by the Registrar General, that the Lancashire operatives, while put upon the distress pittance of food, were actually improving in health, because of their temporary exclusion by the cotton famine from the cotton factory, and that the mortality of the children was decreasing, because their mothers were now at last allowed to give them instead of Godfrey's cordial their own breasts.

Again reverse the medal. The Income and Property Tax Returns, laid before the House of Commons on July 20, 1864, teach us that the persons with yearly incomes, valued by the tax gatherer at £50,000 and upwards, had, from April 5th, 1862, to April 5th, 1863, been joined by a dozen and one, their number having increased in that single year from 67 to 80. The same returns disclose the fact that about 3,000 persons divide amongst themselves a yearly income of about £25,000,000 sterling, rather more than the total revenue doled out annually to the whole mass of the agricultural labourers of England and Wales. Open the Census of 1861, and you will find that the number of the male landed proprietors of England and Wales had decreased from 16,934 in

1851, to 15,066 in 1861, so that the concentration of land had grown in ten years 11 per cent. If the concentration of the soil of the country in a few hands proceed at the same rate, the land question will become singularly simplified, as it had become in the Roman Empire, when Nero grinned at the discovery that half the province of Africa was owned by six gentlemenn.

Wages Have Not Increased

We have dwelt so long upon these "facts so astonishing as to be almost incredible," because England heads the Europe of Commerce and Industry. It will be remembered that some months ago one of the refugee sons of Louis Phillippe [Bonaparte III] publicly congratulated the English agricultural labourer on the superiority of his lot over that of his less florid comrade on the other side of the Channel. Indeed, with local colours changed, and on a scale somewhat contracted, the English facts reproduce themselves in all the industrious and progressive countries of the continent. In all of them there has taken place, since 1848, an unheard-of development of industry, and an undreamed-of expansion of imports and exports. In all of them "the augmentation of wealth and power entirely confined to classes of property" was truly "intoxicating." In all of them, as in England, a minority of the working classes got their real wages somewhat advanced; while in most cases the monetary rise of wages denoted no more a real access of comforts than the inmate of the metropolitan poor-house or orphan asylum, for instance, was in the least benefitted by his first necessaries costing £9 15s. 8d. in 1861 against £7 7s. 4d. in 1952. Everywhere the great mass of the working classes were sinking down to a lower depth, at the same rate at least that those above them were rising in the social scale. In all countries of Europe it has now become a truth demonstrable to every unprejudiced mind, and only denied by those whose interest it is to hedge other people in a fool's paradise, that no improvement of machinery, no appliance of science to production, no contrivances of communication, no new colonies, no emigration, no opening of markets, no free trade, nor all these things put together, will do away with the miseries of the industrious masses; but that, on the present false base, every fresh development of the productive powers of labour must tend to deepen social contrasts and point social antagonisms. Death of starvation rose almost to the rank of an institution, during this intoxicating epoch of economical progress, in the metropolis of the British Empire. That epoch is marked in the annals of the world by the quickened return, the widening compass and the deadlier effects of the social pest called a commercial and industrial crisis.

After the failure of the revolutions of 1848, all party organizations and party journals of the working classes were, on the Continent, crushed by the iron hand of force, the most advanced sons of labour fled in despair to the Transatlantic republic, and the short-lived dreams of emancipation vanished before an epoch of industrial fever, moral marasm, and political reaction. The defeat of the continental working classes, partly owed to the diplomacy of the English Government, acting then as now in fraternal solidarity with the Cabinet of St. Petersburgh, soon spread its contagious effects to this side of the channel. While the rout of their continental brethren unmanned the English working classes, and broke their faith in their own cause, it restored to the landlord and the money lord their somewhat shaken confidence. They insolently withdrew concessions already advertised. The discoveries of new goldlands led to an immense exodus, leaving an irreparable void in the ranks of the British proletariat. Others of its formerly active members were caught by the temporary bribe of greater work and wages, and turned into "political blacks." All the efforts made at keeping up, or remodelling, the Chartist Movement, failed signally, the press organs of the working class died one by one of the apathy of the masses, and, in point of fact, never before seemed the English working class so thoroughly reconciled to a state of political nullity. If, then, there had been no solidarity of action between the British and the continental working classes, there was, at all events, a solidarity of defeat.

Some Progress Is Made

And yet the period passed since the revolutions of 1848 has not been without its compensating features. We shall here only point to two great facts.

After a thirty years' struggle, fought with most admirable perseverance, the English working classes, improving a momentaneous split between the landlords and money lords, succeeded in carrying the Ten Hours' Bill. The immense physical, moral, and intellectual benefits hence accruing to the factory operatives, half yearly chronicled in the reports of the inspectors of factories, are now acknowledged on all sides. Most of the continental governments had to accept the English Factory Act in more or less modified forms, and the English Parliament itself is every year compelled to enlarge its sphere of action. But besides its practical import, there was something else to exalt the marvellous success of this working men's measure. Through their most notorious organs of science . . . the middle class had predicted, and to their hearts' content proved, that any legal restriction of the hours of labour must sound the death knell of British industry, which, vampyre like, could but live by sucking blood, and children's blood, too. In olden times, child murder was a mysterious rite of the religion of Moloch, but it was practised on some very solemn occasions only, once a year perhaps, and then Moloch had no exclusive bias for the children of the poor. This struggle about the legal restriction of the hours of labour raged the more fiercely since apart from frightened avarice, it told indeed upon the great contest between the blind rule of the supply and demand laws which form the political economy of the middle class, and social production controlled by social foresight, which forms the political economy of the working class. Hence the Ten Hours Bill was not only a great practical success; it was the victory of a principle; it was the first time that in broad daylight the political economy of the middle class succumbed to the political economy of the working class.

A Greater Victory for Labour

But there was in store a still greater victory of the political economy of labour, over the political economy of property. We speak of the co-operative movement, especially the co-operative factories raised by the unassisted efforts of a few bold "hands." The value of these great social experiments cannot be over-rated. By deed, instead of by argument, they have shown that production on a large scale, and in accord with the behests of modern science, may be carried on without the existence of a class of masters employing a class of hands; that to bear fruit, the means of labour need not be monopolised as a means of dominion over, and of extortion against, the labouring man himself; and that, like slave labour, like serf labour, hired labour is but a transitory and inferior form, destined to disappear before associated labour plying its toil with a willing hand, a ready mind, and a joyous heart. In England, the seeds of the co-operative system were sown by [Welsh Socialist and philanthropist] Robert Owen; the working men's experiments, tried on the continent, were in fact, the practical upshot of the theories, not invented, but loudly proclaimed in 1848.

The Duty of the Working Classes

At the same time, the experience of the period from 1848 to 1864, has proved beyond doubt, that, however excellent in principle, and however useful in practice, co-operative labour, if kept within the narrow circle of the casual efforts of private workmen, will never be able to arrest the growth in geometrical progression of monopoly, to free the masses nor even to perceptibly lighten the burden of their miseries. It is perhaps for this very reason that plausible noblemen, philanthropic middle class spouters, and even keen political economists, have all at once turned nauscously complimentary to the very co-operative labour system they had vainly tried to nip in the bud by deriding it as the Utopia of the dreamer, or stigmatising it as the sacrilege of the socialist. To save the industrious masses, co-operative labour ought to be developed to national dimensions, and, consequently, to be fostered by national means. Yet the lords of land and the lords of capital will always use their political privileges for the defence and perpetuation of their economical monopolies. So far from promoting, they will continue to lay every possible impediment in the way of the emancipation of labour. Remember the sneer with which, last session, [Prime Minister] Lord Palmerston put down the advocates of the Irish Tenants' Right Bill. The House of Commons, cried he, is a house of landed proprietors. To conquer political power was therefore become the great duty of the working classes. They seem to have comprehended this for in England, Germany, Italy, and France there have taken place simultaneous revivals, and simultaneous efforts are being made at the political reorganisation of the working men's party.

One element of success they possess—numbers; but numbers weigh only in the balance, if united by combination and led by knowledge. Past experience has shown how disregard of that bond of brotherhood which ought to exist between the workmen of different countries, and incite them to stand firmly by each other in all their struggles for emancipation, will be chastised by the common discomfiture of their incoherent efforts. This thought prompted the working men of different countries assembled on September 28, 1864, in public meeting at St. Martin's Hall, to found the International Association.

Another Conviction swayed that meeting.

Slavery Must End

If the emancipation of the working classes requires their fraternal concurrence, how are they to fulfil that great mission with a foreign policy in pursuit of criminal designs, playing upon national prejudices, and squandering in piratical wars the people's blood and treasure? It was not the wisdom of the ruling classes, but the heroic resistance to their criminal folly by the working classes of England that saved the West of Europe from plunging headlong into an infamous crusade for the perpetuation and propagation of slavery on the other side of the Atlantic. The shameless approval, mock sympathy, or idiotic indifference, with which the upper classes of Europe have witnessed the mountain fortress of the Caucasus falling a prey to and heroic Poland being assassinated by Russia; the immense and unresisted encroachments of that barbarous power, whose head is at St. Petersburg, and whose hands are in every Cabinet of Europe, have taught the working classes the duty to master themselves the mysteries of international politics; to watch the diplomatic acts of their respective Governments; to counteract them, if necessary, by all means in their power; when unable to prevent, to combine in simultaneous denunciations, and to vindicate the simple laws of morals and justice, which ought to govern the relations of private individuals, as the rules paramount of the intercourse of nations.

The fight for such a foreign policy forms part of the general struggle for the emancipation of the working classes.

Proletarians of all countries, Unite!

Lee Surrenders at Appomattox and Ends the Civil War: 1865

The Night Before Appomattox

by George Edward Pickett

George Edward Pickett was a major general in the Confederate army and served under General Robert E. Lee. Although he finished last in his class at West Point, he was one of only three to make the rank of general. He is best known for a climactic attack at the Battle of Gettysburg on July 3, 1863, called Pickett's Charge.

In the months leading up to Lee's surrender at Appomattox, Pickett and his men showed great bravery but were ultimately overwhelmed by Union general Philip Henry Sheridan's forces at Five Forks. There, on April 1, 1865, twenty-two thousand Union soldiers under the command of Generals Sheridan and Union general Gouverneur Kemble Warren faced off against ten thousand Confederate soldiers under Pickett's command. After a brave battle during which nearly half of Pickett's men were killed or wounded, General Warren's Fifth Corps overwhelmed them and took many prisoners. Union troops had finally pierced Lee's elaborate defensive line. There had simply been too few men to continue to hold it. The Union victory also threatened the South Side Railroad, Lee's last supply line into Petersburg. It would only be a matter of days before Lee faced Union general Ulysses S. Grant at Appomattox Court House to sign the surrender agreement that brought an end to the bloodiest war ever fought on American soil.

Although Pickett was much criticized, Lee retained him in divisional command throughout the Virginia Campaign of 1864. In the following letter that General Pickett wrote to his wife on the eve of the surrender at Appomattox, he describes the events at Five Forks and how his soldiers acted in fierce bravery in the face of overwhelming odds.

George Edward Pickett, *The Night Before Appomattox*, April 8, 1865.

Tomorrow, my darling, may see our flag furled forever. Jack-
erie, our faithful old mail-carrier, sobs behind me as I write.
He bears to-night this—his last—message from me as "Our
Cupid." First he is commissioned with three orders, which I
know you will obey as fearlessly as the bravest of your brother
soldiers. Keep up a stout heart. Believe that I shall come back to
you and know that God reigns. After to-night you will be my
whole command—staff, field officers, men—all. The second
commission is only given as a precaution—lest I should not return or lest for some time I should not be with you.

Lee's surrender is imminent. It is finished. Through the suggestion for their commanding officers as many of the men as desire are permitted to cut through and join [General Joseph] Johnston's army. The cloud of despair settled over all on the third,
when the tidings came to us of the evacuation of Richmond and
its partial loss by fire. The homes and families of many of my
men were there, and all knew too well that with the fall of our
Capital the last hope of success was over. And yet, my beloved,
these men as resolutely obeyed the orders of their commanding
officers as if we had captured and burned the Federal Capital.

The horrors of the march from Five Forks to Amelia Court
House and thence to Sailor's Creek beggars all description. For
forty-eight hours the man or officer who had a handful of parched
corn in his pocket was most fortunate. We reached Sailor's Creek
on the morning of the sixth, weary, starving, despairing.

[Union general Philip] Sheridan was in our front, delaying us
with his cavalry (as was his custom) until the infantry should
come up. [Confederate general William] Mahone was on our
right, [Confederate general Richard] Ewell on our left. Mahone
was ordered to move on, and we ordered to stand still. The movement of Mahone left a gap which increased as he went on. [Gen-
eral] Huger's battalion of artillery, in attempting to cross the gap,
was being swept away when I pushed on with two of my
brigades across Sailor's Creek.

We formed line of battle across an open field, holding it
against repeated charges of Sheridan's dismounted cavalry. At
about three o'clock the infantry which Sheridan had been looking for came up, completely hemming us in. [General] Anderson
ordered me to draw off my brigades to the rear and to cut our
way out in any possible manner that we could. [General] Wise's
Brigade was deployed in the rear to assist us, but was charged

upon all sides by the enemy and, though fighting manfully to the last, was forced to yield. Two of my brigadiers, Corse and Hunton, were taken prisoners. The other two barely escaped, and my life, by some miracle, was spared. And by another miracle, greater still, I escaped capture. A squadron of the enemy's cavalry was riding down upon us, two of my staff and myself, when a small squad of my men recognized me and, risking their own lives, rallied to our assistance and suddenly delivered a last volley into the faces of the pursuing horsemen, checking them but for a moment. But in that one moment we, by the speed of our horses, made our escape. Ah, my darling, the sacrifice of this little band of men is like unto that which was made at Calvary.

It is finished! Ah, my beloved division! Thousands of them have gone to their eternal home, having given up their lives for the cause they knew to be just. The others, alas, heart-broken, crushed in spirit, are left to mourn its loss. Well, it is practically all over now. We have poured out our blood and suffered untold hardships and privations all in vain. And now, well, I must not forget, either, that God reigns. Life is given us for the performance of duty, and duty performed is happiness.

It is finished—the suffering, the horrors, the anguish of these last hours of struggle. The glorious gift of your love will help me to bear the memory of them. In this midnight hour I feel the caressing blessing of your pure spirit as it mingles with mine. Peace is born.

From now forever only
YOUR SOLDIER.

The Road to Reunion

by Robert Hendrickson

The American Civil War lasted nearly five years and cost the country more than seven hundred thousand lives, more than all subsequent American wars combined. A large percentage of casualties tragically occurred in the final months before General Robert E. Lee's surrender. After a year of bloody skirmishes over control of the Confederate capital of Richmond, Virginia, General Lee finally opened up correspondence with Union general Ulysses S. Grant. Two days later, on April 9, 1865, the Union army and General Grant finally achieved their main objective: the surrender of Confederate general Robert E. Lee's army. Grant and Lee met in a private home behind the courthouse in the sleepy Virginia village of Appomattox, where Lee signed the documents surrendering his army. Lee's surrender marked the end of major hostilities. By the end of May, all fighting was over. The Civil War had ended, and the work of rebuilding the nation had begun.

In the end, the Confederate army was severely weakened by hunger, exhaustion, disease, and an epidemic of desertions. Many Confederate soldiers taken prisoner by the Union army in the final months did not even have shoes. The Civil War changed America in many ways. The slaves were emancipated, and the economy had to be rebuilt. Southern states once joined in the Confederacy were now at odds. The war was very costly, and many homes and plantations were destroyed. Families were torn apart, and thousands of freed slaves emigrated north and entered the labor force.

The following essay by Robert Hendrickson describes the immediate effects of Lee's surrender at Appomattox Court House and the end of one of America's most tragic conflicts. Hendrickson has received Ford Foundation and McDowell Colony fellowships. His articles have appeared widely in newspapers and literary quarterlies. He is the author of more than forty books, including *Sumter: The First Days of the Civil War.*

I t rained the next day in Appomattox, but on that April 10 morning at nine o'clock General [Ulysses] Grant and his staff rode out to confer with General [Robert E.] Lee again on a knoll overlooking both their lines, Lee galloping out alone to meet him when Grant arrived a little early. This meeting in the drizzling rain had been arranged at [the home of Wilmer] McLean's the day before and the two generals withdrew to discuss privately matters Grant knew exceeded his authority from Lincoln but which he felt morally bound to pursue. He did tell Horace Porter and the rest of his staff the gist of the conversation.

Porter recalled years after the event that both generals in their half-hour talk had expressed a hope that the war would soon be over. Lee told Grant there was no reason good relations could not be restored between North and South—not even the issue of slavery, which most Southerners no longer supported. He believed that all remaining Confederate armies should surrender, "as nothing could be gained by further resistance in the field," but he refrained from promising Grant that he would try to influence [Confederate president] Jefferson Davis or anyone else about such a surrender. Porter insisted that Grant never asked Lee to consult with President [Abraham] Lincoln concerning the terms of reconstruction. "After the conversation," he wrote, "the two commanders lifted their hats and said good-bye. Lee rode back to his camp to take a final farewell of his army, and Grant returned to McLean's house, where he seated himself on the porch until it was time to take his final departure."

Later, on April 20, Lee did write Jefferson Davis, urging the fleeing president to cease all hostilities:

> From what I have seen and learned, I believe an army cannot be organized or supported in Virginia, and as far as I know the condition of affairs, the country east of the Mississippi is morally and physically unable to maintain the contest unaided with any hope of ultimate success. A partisan [guerrilla] war may be contained,

and hostilities protracted, causing individual suffering and the devastation of the country, but I see no prospect by that means of achieving separate independence. . . . To save useless effusion of blood, I would recommend measures be taken for suspension and the restoration of peace.

No Confederate Army Is Left

It will probably never be known whether Grant asked Lee to visit President Lincoln, as Colonel Marshall—Porter to the contrary—insisted that Lee told *him*. But Lee almost certainly advised Grant that his campaign in Virginia was "the last organized resistance which the South was capable of making—that . . . there was no longer any [Confederate] army which could make a stand." This Grant told his biographer John Russell Young years later, and it was the prevalent opinion North and South when the two commanders said good-bye that last time. Many more men would die after Appomattox, there were still armies in the field and Davis's government remained at large, but for all practical purposes the Civil War was over.

When Lee left Grant and rode back to camp he came upon a Union general, an old adversary of many battles. "Don't you know me, General Lee?" the man asked. "I'm George Meade."

"Oh, is that you, Meade?" Lee replied. "How did you get all that gray in your beard?"

"I'm afraid you're the cause of most of it," Meade laughed. The two rode together for a distance, across the ravine separating the Union forces from the shattered remains of the Confederate army. Meade ordered his color-bearer to unfurl the Stars and Stripes, riding past cheering men, including one proud and bitter Confederate veteran who cried out, "Damn your old rag! We are cheering General Lee!"

More typical were the Southerners who came over to the Federal lines to visit with their old adversaries. "We were glad to see them," Union private Theodore Gerrish recalled. "We received them kindly, and exchanged pocket knives and sundry trinkets, that each could have something to carry home as a reminiscence of the great event." However, a friendly wrestling match between a Billy Yank and a Johnny Reb is said to have resulted in the final death at Appomattox. The winner, according to the traditional tale, was General Lee's cook, Confederate champion Captain Joel Compton.

The Celebration Is in Full Swing

Lee had his general pass to leave now. Dated Appomattox Court House, Virginia, April 10, 1865, it was signed by Grant and read:

> All officers commanding posts, pickets or detachments will pass General R.E. Lee through their lines north or south on presentation of this pass. General Lee will be permitted to visit Richmond at any time, unless otherwise ordered by competent authority, and every facility for his doing so will be given by officers of the United States Army to whom this may be presented.

A Confederate soldier who saw Lee leaving wrote, "We who live today shall never see his like again, and whether our posterity does is problematical."

General Robert E. Lee, who would always be in the South of that day the Lancelot of all knights, the courtliest knight that ever bare shield, the kindliest man that ever strake with sword, the goodliest person that ever came among press of knights. The gray knight, the great patriarch, Uncle Robert, left Appomattox aboard the faithful Traveler toward eleven o'clock, attended by a single servant. Fatigued and bent over slightly, no longer ramrod straight in the saddle, he was on his way to Richmond and his ailing wife, who had aged as much as he had during the war, face gaunt, hair white—from the fields of war into the vales of peace.

Grant the great commoner chatted pleasantly on the McLean porch with passersby and General "Pete" Longstreet, who had been an attendant at his wedding, among other old Southern friends. "Why do men fight who were born to be brothers?" Longstreet later mused on recalling the meeting. Grant refused to go back to Richmond, according to his wife's memoirs, because he didn't want to distress the people there and add to their despair. The Union commander departed at about noon for City Point, where Julia waited for her "Victor," and then on to Washington to see President Lincoln for the last time before his assassination. Neither he nor Lee would be present at the formal Appomattox surrender ceremony that Grant had insisted upon, which was scheduled for April 12. Even as the two generals went their separate ways from Appomattox, the greatest celebration in the history of the country was in full swing.

PEACE! THE BLOODSHED ENDED!
WHOLE REBEL ARMY SURRENDERS!

VICTORY!

PEACE!

So read newspaper headlines across the nation. The celebrating had begun the evening before in Washington when Grant's telegram was received, a cable that brought "news from Heaven," as New England poet James Russell Lowell put it in a letter to a friend, Harvard professor Charles Eliot Norton. Barely mentioned were the casualties of the Appomattox campaign: 1,316 Union dead, 7,750 wounded; 1,200 Confederate dead, 6,000 wounded. The tidings of joy spread from great city to tiny rural hamlet as reporters wired their stories through the night, often with a glass or bottle of whiskey in hand.

In Richmond, despite Grant's orders, guns boomed and shattered windows. In Washington a five-hundred-gun dawn salute was ordered by [U.S. secretary of war Edwin] Stanton; howitzers sounded from the Navy Yard, flares and fireworks lit the sky. There was no work that Monday except on the premises of Ebenezer Scrooges. All government offices were closed, and the whole city seemed to have taken to the streets from early morning on. Bands playing "Yankee Doodle," "Rally 'Round the Flag Boys," "Marching Through Georgia," and a dozen more popular songs marched down Pennsylvania Avenue, followed by crowds of people singing and cheering and waving flags.

Celebrations in the North

A group of Treasury workers marched to the White House and serenaded President Lincoln with "Praise God from Whom All Blessings Flow" and "The Star-Spangled Banner" while he tried to eat his breakfast. Toward noon a crowd of over three thousand gathered at the White House and cheered wildly, especially when young Tad [Lincoln] waved one of his collection of captured Confederate battle flags from a window. Without making a formal speech, a tired President Lincoln joked with the revelers and asked their three bands to join together and play "Dixie" because, although the South had always claimed it, "yesterday . . . we fairly captured it" and "it is one of the best tunes I have ever heard." Then he led the crowd, waving his big hands, in three cheers for General Grant and his men.

It was the same all over the North. "All, all are jubilant," wrote Secretary of the Navy Gideon Welles in his diary for the day. In

Chicago bells pealed and a one-hundred-cannon salute awakened the city; throngs of people surged through the streets with torches. In New York City a gathering of twenty thousand businessmen sang "Praise God," the psalm of thanksgiving; flags waved from windows in mansions and tenements—the entire supply of flags in the city was said to be sold out. GOOD NEWS! LEE AND THE WHOLE REBEL ARMY SURRENDER! one newspaper headline screamed. Diarist George Templeton Strong wrote for his Monday, April 10, entry: "Lee and his army have surrendered. Gloria in excelsis Deo! They can bother and perplex none but historians henceforth, forever. There is no such army anymore. God be praised!"

Sometimes the celebrating went too far. "Dear Wife," wrote I. Shoger, a mud-marcher with [Union general Philip] Sheridan's army. "[We] got the news of Lee's capture . . . you aught to have seen the excitement. The dispatch was redd by Genl. Sherman in front of the [Smithfield] Court house. Our band was at the head of the collume, we playd all the National airs, the soldiers threw up thair hats and chreed with all thair might. They got a negro on a blanket and threw him ten feet [in the air]."

GLORIOUS NEWS IS RECEIVED, blared another headline. Throughout the land cannons sounded, shotguns blasted, pistols cracked, men galloped wildly on horses, wagons full of people raced down the streets cheering, church bells and cathedral bells and school bells rang out wildly and unceasingly, flag-bedecked riverboats sounded their whistles, fire engines blanketed with flags roared and whistled down grand avenues and dirt roads, saloon keepers poured free beer for everyone until they ran out of it. Anything that could make noise, from bands and firecrackers to women banging on pots and pans and burly men banging with sledgehammers on giant boilers, was brought out into the streets. Never did so many flags wave in the nation's history, even though half the country wasn't waving any. Enemies shook hands and strangers hugged each other. Those against the war and those for the war all joined in rejoicing that the war was over, and all cried that Monday as they celebrated. People from every walk of life—from doctors and lawyers to foundry workers and porters—shouted: "The war is over! Hurrah for Grant! Hurrah for Lincoln! The boys are coming home!" No longer was America a house divided or a slaughterhouse. No longer did "the evil of slavery stain America's escutcheon," as General Theodore Gates put it, "she stood before the world in the sublime majesty of a nation free in fact, as well as theory."

It lasted all that day: the shouting and singing and dancing in the streets, the torchlight parades and bonfires, the men and women marching, turning somersaults and walking on their hands, standing upright atop their horses, swinging from trees and lampposts. It lasted into the next day until the exhausted celebrants finally turned to more somber forms of thanksgiving like Grand Illumination Night in Washington, when thousands of people put lighted candles in their windows.

A Formal Surrender

Back in Appomattox Court House one final ceremony had to be performed. General Grant had insisted upon it against Confederate wishes—a formal surrender, the traditional laying down of arms. The official ceremony was essential, Grant had held, lest any of the country ever forget. To some such a ceremony seemed divisive, but as it happened it became the crowning glory of the spirit of reconciliation fostered at Appomattox, a surging tide of brotherhood that would begin to ebb when Lincoln died three days later of his assassin's bullet.

Grant had set the formal surrender for the morning of Wednesday April 12 and selected the Union hero Brigadier General Joshua Chamberlain to command the ceremony. Lee had appointed the brave Georgian General John B. Gordon to lead the column of Confederate troops across the valley from their broken encampment and up the road leading through Appomattox, where erect Union soldiers lined each side of the street. Behind Gordon in the gray column that chill gray morning were the two hundred survivors of the once mighty Stonewall Brigade, and behind their ragged unit marched thousands more men.

Remembering the spectacle, Chamberlain wrote:

On they come with the old swinging route step and swaying battle-flags . . . crowded so thick, by the thinning out of men, that the whole column seemed crowned with red. . . . Before us in proud humiliation stood the embodiment of manhood: men whom neither toils nor sufferings, nor the fact of death, nor disaster, nor hopelessness could bend from their resolve; standing before us now, thin, worn, and famished, but erect, and with eyes looking level into ours, waking memories that bound us together as no other bond—was not such manhood to be welcomed back into a Union so tested and assured?

General Gordon at the head of the tramping column seemed to ride "with heavy spirit and downcast face," his officers grim, expecting the worst humiliation from Chamberlain, Rebel bullet holes ventilating his Yankee coat. But then Gordon heard from the Union lines the order for the marching salute, a bugle sounding the same order, the clatter of thousands of Union muskets raised to the shoulder in the "carry" salute to a respected enemy. Gordon knew immediately what this meant and turned toward Chamberlain, wheeled smartly, "making with himself and his horse one uplifted figure," raised his sword and as the horse dipped brought his sword down to his boot tip, saluting Chamberlain before he shouted an order for all the advancing Confederates to return the Union tribute to their courage. It was "honor answering honor," Chamberlain said. "On our part not a sound of trumpet more, nor roll of drums; not a cheer, nor word, nor whisper of vain-glorying, nor motion of man standing again at the order, but an awed stillness rather, and breath-holding, as if it were the passing of the dead."

With each unit that passed came the memory of terrible battles in which both victor and vanquished had fought: Bull Run . . . Shiloh . . . Gettysburg . . . Chickamauga . . . The Wilderness . . . Cold Harbor . . . Five Forks. There were tears on both sides. "Many of the grizzled veterans wept like women," a Confederate officer recalled. "My own eyes were as blind as my voice was dumb." Then came the most painful part of the ceremony for the worn, half-starved men in gray. Wrote Chamberlain:

> They fix bayonets, stack arms, then, hesitatingly, remove cartridge-boxes and lay them down. Lastly, reluctantly, with agony of expression—they tenderly fold their flags, battle-worn and torn, blood-stained, heart-holding colors, and lay them down, some frenziedly rushing from the ranks, kneeling over them, clinging to them, pressing them to their lips with burning tears. And only the Flag of the Union greets the sky!

Left with Haunted Memories

After the last parole, a bitter Confederate officer, apparently made mad by the war, told Chamberlain, "You may forgive us, General, but we won't be *forgiven*. There is a rancor in our hearts which you little dream of. We *hate* you, sir!" But most were consoled by the ceremony and would stand upon their honor. "I fear we would not have done the same by you had the situation been reversed," said one Rebel officer. Said a North Carolinian: "I will go home and tell Joe Johnston we can't fight men such as you. I will advise him to surrender." Still another officer pointed to the Stars and Stripes. "We had our choice of weapons and of ground and we have lost," he said. "Now that is my flag, and I will prove myself as worthy as any of you."

By the next day the nearly twenty-eight thousand Confederates were paroled and departing the battlefield. "A strange and somber shadow rose up ghostlike from the haunts of memory or habit and rested down on the final parting scene," Chamberlain remembered. "How strange the undertone of sadness even at the release from prison and from pain! It seems as if we had put some precious part of ourselves there which we are loath to leave. When all is over . . . the long lines of scattered cartridges are set on fire and the lurid flames wreathing the blackness of earthly shadows give an unearthly border to our parting."

Recalled Confederate soldier Barry Benson: "So Blackwood and I left the army, our army, left them there on the hill with their arms stacked in the field all in rows, never to see them anymore. . . . We crossed the road into the field into the thickets and in a little while lost sight of all that was left of the army." Confederate Carlton McCarthy wrote: "Comrades wept as they gazed upon each other and with choking voices said farewell. And so— they parted. Little groups of two or three or four, without food, without money, but with the satisfaction that proceeds from the consciousness of duty faithfully performed, were soon plodding their way homeward."

Behind them they left comrades in the field hospitals. Hundreds, thousands who would never make the journey home alive. An observer at nearby Burkesville Hospital wrote:

> Three thousand men were lying in this squalid suffering. In one row were five men lying on a hard floor . . . all dying. Two of them were conscious and were able to gasp out last words for wife or mother which were quickly written down. . . . In a small room were three hopeless cases, placed there that they might breathe their last in peace apart from the noise and excitement—one with a shell wound through both his hips, another with an arm and

shoulder carried away, and the other with his jaw and face terribly shattered and his tongue half gone.

But the lucky ones could not look back. They headed home down dusty roads and through green pastures filled with blue chicory, dandelions, Queen Anne's lace, purple crown vetch, hawkweed, all the lovely escapes or weed flowers of the country. Absent were the hundreds of thousands who had fallen on ten thousand such fields. With some went comrades crippled, blinded, made insane or almost so; they would be joined by others like them along the way, by men with their names and addresses pinned to them so that they could be delivered by kind strangers to their homes, by men released from prison camps whose eyes bulged out and whose skeletons had worked through. No simple country lads of yesterday were going home—the country lads were all dead in one way or another.

Chamberlain, who was looking on, would later write: "Over all the hillsides in the peaceful sunshine, are clouds of men on foot or horse, singly or in groups, making their earnest way, as if by the instinct of an ant, each with his own little burden, each for his own little house."

Many burdens were far from little, but they weren't soldiers anymore; they were no longer armies. "The charges were now withdrawn from the guns," Horace Porter recalled, "the campfires were left to smoulder in their ashes, the flags were tenderly furled—those historic banners, battle-stained, bullet-riddled . . . with scarcely enough left of them on which to imprint the names of the battles they had seen—and the Army of the Union and the Army of Northern Virginia turned their backs upon each other for the first time in four long bloody years."

The Rise of the Paris Commune Signals Future Violent Revolution

by Robert Tombs

In 1871 France went to war with Prussia and was defeated. Having faced a four-month-long Prussian siege of the city that resulted in devastating famine and disease, the citizens of Paris were outraged over the concessions that Louis-Adolphe Thiers, president of the French National Assembly, made with Prussian chancellor Otto von Bismarck while negotiating the peace treaty that ended the war. Regaining control of Paris and convincing the city that the war with Prussia was over was impossible for Thiers. The French National Guard refused to disarm against Thiers's newly assembled national government, and a bitter civil war broke out in Paris. The revolution succeeded, and Thiers's national government abandoned the city. The Parisians organized a provisional proletariat government composed of ordinary citizens, revolutionaries, Socialists, and laborers called the Paris Commune. The citizens who supported the commune were known as Communards, and they numbered in the tens of thousands.

The Paris Commune ruled the city for seventy-two days, and it was the first time in history that a proletariat government had ever been in power. It had dreams of justice and created legislation to re-

Robert Tombs, "The Paris Commune," *History Review*, September 1999, p. 36. Copyright
© 1999 by History Today, Ltd. Reproduced by permission.

store the rights of exploited and disinherited laborers and citizens. It also destroyed monuments in the city that celebrated Napoléon's bourgeois, oppressive republic, including Theirs's house and the Vendome Column in the center of the city, which commemorated Napoléon I's victories. The Paris Commune was the first revolution in which the working class played a central role and sought to change society for the better.

Finally, after seventy-two days, Thiers's Versailles troops stormed Paris and used cannon fire to cross the city. There was massive chaos. Over the following week there would be so much violent destruction that it would come to be known as "La Semaine Sanglante" ("The Week of Blood"). Led by Thiers, the Versailles army rounded up prisoners against city walls and slaughtered them by the thousands. The commune eventually succumbed to defeat. To this day it is not known how many Communards were executed, killed in street fighting, or summarily shot down, but the estimated count is near ten thousand. Even today, the Communards are commemorated in an annual celebration held by French Socialists at the site where most of the Communards were executed.

In the following essay Robert Tombs explains why the Paris Commune of 1871, which ended in the most ferocious outbreak of civil violence in nineteenth-century Europe, is still a subject of intense historical interest and controversy. Tombs is a reader in French history at Cambridge University and a fellow of St. John's College.

Before daybreak on 18 March 1871, several thousand cold and miserable French troops trudged up the steep streets of Montmartre, the hill overlooking northern Paris, to capture by surprise hundreds of cannon parked on the summit by dissident units of the Paris National Guard, the citizen militia. Seizing these heavy weapons was to be the first step towards reimposing the national government's authority on the unruly capital. Since the beginning of the war with Germany [the Franco-Prussian War] the previous July, which had led to a four-month siege of the city, Parisians had become increasingly disaffected from their rulers. The end of the war had left Paris ungovernable, as most of the regular army was demobilised while the National Guard kept its guns. The newly elected National Assembly, which had a royalist majority, was far away in Bordeaux. The government it appointed, led by Louis-Adolphe Thiers, intended to assert its authority over Paris. The Montmartre expedition was the outcome.

It led to one of the most famous, and fateful, scenes in French history. Thousands of local National Guards, together with women and children, turned out to obstruct and argue with the outnumbered and visibly unenthusiastic soldiers. The streets became jammed with people, horses and cannon. A few shots were fired by both sides, but generally the soldiers ignored their officers' orders to force back the crowds. Some handed over their rifles and went off arm in arm, fraternising and singing with the civilians. Two generals were grabbed by the crowd and later shot in a neighbouring back yard.

Across the city, people threw up barricades, as in 1848 and 1830. The government and the army high command, convinced that they had lost control, retreated with all available troops to Versailles, ten miles south-west of Paris, where the National Assembly arrived from Bordeaux on 20 March. The Central Committee of the Republican Federation of the Paris National Guard—an unofficial body set up in February to co-ordinate the activity of the militia battalions, hence their popular name of 'Federes' established a provisional authority at the Hotel de Ville, the city hall.

A week later, elections in which over a quarter of a million voters took part chose a city council mainly composed of revolutionaries; veteran democrats from 1848, radical journalists, labour militants, and patriotic National Guards who assumed the title of Paris Commune. 'Commune', the French term for the basic unit of local government, signified grass-roots democracy, and also consciously recalled the first revolutionary Paris Commune of 1792; it did not imply communism. The red flag and the 1793 revolutionary calendar were adopted, according to which they were in Germinal Year 79. The proclamation of the Commune was a joyous popular ceremony, described by the writer Jules Valles (a member of the Commune) as "calm and beautiful as a blue river." The cheering, singing and marching crowds believed that the 'Free City of Paris' would begin a new era as a democratic and social republic. Every previous insurrection that had successfully gained control of Paris had gone on to rule France.

The Origins of the Commune

The roots of the Commune lay in the Parisian 'revolutionary tradition', which had already overthrown conservative regimes in
1830 and 1848. Many Parisians aspired to an egalitarian democratic and social republic. Republicanism had been revived by
campaigns against Emperor Napoleon III in the late 1860s. It was
radicalised by the effects of the disastrous Franco-Prussian War
(July 1870–January 1871), which led to a rapid and unstoppable
German invasion of France. The defeated emperor was overthrown in a republican revolution on 4 September 1870, but the
moderate republican government that replaced him managed neither to defeat the Germans nor to negotiate with them. The invaders besieged Paris from September 1870 to January 1871.
Parisians were armed and enrolled in a mass National Guard.
Starved into surrender, they angrily blamed the government for
their defeat. Moreover, they were determined to preserve the Republic from a possible monarchist restoration. The events of
Montmartre detonated this already explosive situation.

The new Commune represented the left wing of Parisian politics. About half were middle-class (journalists, lawyers, small
businessmen, master craftsmen), and the other half white-collar
workers or skilled manual workers, often labour leaders, from the
main Paris trades (metal-working, jewellery, furniture, clothing
etc). It is noteworthy that among this heterogeneous group there
was not a single unskilled labourer. Unlike in earlier revolutions,
they were not national politicians; few had more than a local reputation. The better known include the elderly neo-Jacobin journalist Charles Delescluze, the socialist bookbinder Eugene Varlin,
and the painter Gustave Courbet. The aims of the Commune leaders were above all to defend the Republic and to assert the autonomy of Paris as the republican capital. Their immediate acts were
aimed at those they saw as the republic's enemies: the Catholic
Church (which was disestablished), the regular army (which was
abolished, at least for Paris), the police and the bureaucracy, which
were to be democratised and turned over to ordinary citizens—a
project which barely got off the ground. In the free and somewhat
anarchic atmosphere, grass-roots initiatives were permitted and
encouraged, especially in education and the arts.

The Commune's supporters, usually known as 'Communards'
or 'Communeux', were broadly 'the people': the manual and
white-collar wage-earners, self-employed craft workers and small

business people who composed the majority of Parisians. They were comparable with participants in earlier revolutions in 1848, 1830 and even the 1790s. One described himself as follows:

> I am the son of a good patriot of 1792. . . . Journeyman cabinet-maker at 18 years old . . . working during the day, studying at night, history, travels, political and social economy making propaganda and taking part in all republican movements. Arriving in Paris in 1854, two years later I set myself up as a furniture restorer. I employed 1 to 3 workers, paying them 50 centimes per day above the official rate and propagandizing them too. In politics I want the broadest possible sovereignty of the People [and] all the Reforms our defective social and political organization demands.

Women of the Commune

Women played a much-remarked role. They were prominent on 18 March, when the insurrection began. Later, led by activists such as Nathalie Le Mel, Louise Michel (subsequently a well-known anarchist) and the Russian Elisveta Tomanovskaya, they were public speakers, organisers of co-operatives and schools, military nurses and—so conservatives alleged—wielders of rifles and petrol-bombs. There is some debate as to how extensive and how new their activity really was; but it has recently been argued that the Commune marked a new stage in women's political assertiveness.

Given expectations of what revolutions were like, this one seemed remarkably calm, even somnolent, at first. Noted one visiting Englishman, "The first thing that struck me on my arrival was the extreme tranquillity of the streets." The city's tangible calm was partly because much of the administrative machinery ran as usual. It was also because many thousands of middle-class Parisians had left. Others continued to flee, especially men of military age determined to avoid fighting for the Commune or taking the risk of opposing it: some bribed sentries to let them shin down the city ramparts. Others kept off the streets. Consequently, the city centre and residential western quarters, wrote a British visitor, were like 'London on a wet Sunday'. It is harder to find contemporary impressions of the working-class districts where the Commune had most of its supporters. An English journalist, after stressing the emptiness of the city centre, described Montmartre as 'full of life, the shops open, and the streets thronged with women and children—many of the men would have been on military duty. At the Place du Trone the usual Gingerbread Fair was held, with 'nearly as many booths as usual, and acrobats, conjurers, fat ladies and other monstrosities were not wanting'.

Dramatic Acts of Destruction

There were also more political entertainments. Acts of ceremonial destruction were staged to signal the defeat, at least symbolically, of the people's enemies, and these became more spectacular as the situation deteriorated and morale needed a boost. On 6 April, National Guards from the La Roquette district burnt the guillotine taken from its shed near the local prison. Several churches were systematically wrecked. An exhibition in May of human remains discovered in the crypt of Saint-Laurent church and said to be those of girls raped and murdered by the priests, one of several occurrences of anticlerical street-theatre, attracted crowds of sightseers. On 15 May Thiers's house was demolished by decree of the Commune as a reprisal for Versaillais bombardment of the city. On 16 May occurred the most spectacular demolition, which caused world-wide interest: that of the Vendome Column, in the centre of the city, which commemorated Napoleon I's victories.

Economic reforms were far less dramatic. They principally encouraging workers' co-operatives, forbidding night work in bakeries, cancelling war-time rent arrears and returning small items free from the municipal pawnshops. These were seen by some at the time (and by many later commentators) as social experiments of great significance. But there was never any question of seizing private business or financial institutions, such as the Bank of France. Karl Marx criticised this as timidity, but few French socialists favoured state control of an economy still dominated by small businesses. The Commune's only clear ideological split, on 1 May, was over whether to hand emergency dictatorial powers to a five-man Committee of Public Safety (another reference to the 1790s). The majority, mainly neo-Jacobins and followers of the authoritarian revolutionary Auguste Blanqui, voted in favour, against a minority, mainly socialists, who opposed on grounds of democratic principle.

Chaos or Festival?

The life of the Commune was dominated not by ideology or legislation, but by civil war. Skirmishes began on 1 April 1871. A

Parisian march on Versailles on 3 April failed. The Versaillais regular army began siege operations on 11 April. For the rest of April and May, the Commune faced the huge task of organising, arming, equipping, feeding, paying and leading its part-time democratic citizen army in continuous fighting in the suburbs against ever-increasing numbers of Versaillais, who eventually totalled 130,000 men. Most contemporaries and historians have emphasised the disorganisation and indiscipline of the Federes, about 170,000 strong on paper; but, given the improvised and largely voluntary character of their effort, a balanced picture would give more credit to their two-month defence. They were aided by Paris's massive fortifications and the huge stock of weaponry built up during the German siege. Nevertheless, chances of survival were slim: they could not defeat the regular army in battle; they had no significant help from the rest of France (sympathetic uprisings in Marseilles, Lyons, Toulouse and other cities were quickly extinguished); and the German army was camped in their rear, ready to intervene if required. The Versaillais and the Germans contemplated imposing a blockade, but it was never seriously implemented. Food therefore remained available at only slightly higher prices, and Parisians were not again reduced, as under the German siege, to horsemeat and rats.

Life during the Commune has often been portrayed as either chaos or festival, which may be different ways of describing the same things. The first element was the absence of usual routines linked with work, due to the interruption of normal economic life and the subsistence of most working-class Parisians on National Guard pay and rations. Except for usually brief periods of duty, this left most men with free time for socialising, politics and (an accompaniment to both) drinking. The second element was the weakness or absence of conventional authority from above, as public order was largely in the hands of the National Guards themselves and their elected officers. This meant an overturning of the usual hierarchy: middle-class people could be ordered around by workers, which sometimes involved harassment by the officious, the bullying and the drunk. It also meant a much-criticised level of disorganisation, with much arguing and milling around. But it also meant an unprecedented level of freedom and equality. The third element was the decentralisation of initiative, which created a wonderful opportunity for political enthusiasts to make speeches, to run clubs, committees and newspapers, and to take practical action—whether starting co-operatives, opening schools or wrecking churches. Fourth, ignorance of much that was happening inside and especially outside the city meant that both friends and enemies of the Commune had little notion of how long it would last and what the outcome of the conflict might be. For all these reasons, the period from March to May seemed outside normal time. The sentimental way of describing it after the event was as 'le temps des cerises' (cherry time) the title of a song written by a member of the Commune, Jean-Baptiste Clement.

Blood, Destruction, and Myth

Cherry time came brutally to an end on 21 May, when the first Versaillais troops clambered over the shell-torn south-western ramparts. By the next morning, over 100,000 men had overrun the western districts of the city, capturing thousands of Federes almost without resistance. The troops were acclaimed as liberators by throngs of mainly middle-class residents, who showered them with money, food and wine. The atmosphere soon changed in what was to be known as 'La Semaine Sanglante' (Bloody Week), the most deadly and destructive few days in the history of Paris and most ferocious outbreak of civil violence in Europe between the French Revolution of the 1790s and the Bolshevik revolution of 1917. . . . It was like an appalling level-crossing accident at the end of a school outing to the seaside. The disaster would give the Commune a new legend and meaning. From being a rather timid, incompetent and verbose municipal revolution, it became an epic of popular heroism and sacrifice. A sympathetic critic put it bluntly: "The Commune, which would have sunk amid ridicule, took on a tragic dignity."

The Versaillais troops, in overwhelming number, used cannon fire to smash their way across the city from west to east. Several thousand Federe diehards built hundreds of street barricades. Some began to set fire to buildings, first to slow the Versaillais advance, later as a reaction to defeat. Symbolic monuments were gutted, badly damaged or narrowly rescued from the flames, including the Tuileries Palace, the City Hall, the Palace of Justice, the Finance Ministry, the Louvre and Notre Dame. Panicky rumours spread that the Communards were trying to destroy the whole city, and that women fire-raisers (petroleuses) were burning private houses. This along with the pent-up fear and anger the Commune had respired over the previous weeks, led to an increasingly savage reaction against Communard prisoners and suspects. Neighbours denounced each other to the troops; landlords denounced tenants, and shopkeepers, customers.

The Versailles army slaughtered prisoners by the hundred. Often, being wounded, having a recently-fired gun, a right shoulder bruised by the kick of a rifle butt, gunpowder stains or any other suspicious characteristic meant summary execution. Mass slaughter continued for some days in public parks, behind prison walls and most notoriously in the Pere Lachaise cemetery against what is now known as the 'Federes' Wall'. Angry Federes shot several dozen hostages in retaliation, including the Archbishop of Paris. The last flickers of resistance in the working-class eastern quarters were stamped out on 28 May. Convoys of Federe prisoners were mobbed as they were marched off to Versailles. The number of Communards, or suspected Communards, killed in the street fighting, summarily shot down or executed after hasty court-martial will probably never be known for certain. At least 10,000 bodies are known to have been buried in Paris as a result, but most historians assume the total to have been much higher. Many conservatives applauded the carnage as the way to guarantee a generation of peace. This intensity of civil violence was unique in Europe between the French and Russian revolutions, and it left deep scars. To this day an annual commemoration is held by French socialists at the Federes' Wall.

The Significance of the Commune

The Commune has been variously interpreted. The first and most influential commentator was [German political philosopher] Karl Marx, busy in London as events unfolded sending advice to contacts in Paris and formulating reasons why the Commune was an event of historic significance. He and his followers hailed it as the dawn of the age of proletarian revolution and the pioneer of a new form of popular revolutionary government, the dictatorship of the proletariat. They praised the courage of its martyrs, and the song *L'Internationale.* written by Commune member Eugene Pottier, became their revolutionary anthem. In the years that followed, the lesson of the Commune was a bone of contention between socialists who implicitly or explicitly abandoned revolution in favour of electoral politics and trade unionism, and those who insisted that violent revolution was the only route to socialism. Marx and especially [Russian Communist leader Vladimir] Lenin argued that the Commune's failure proved the need for less decency, more ruthlessness and more disciplined leadership in the future. The Communards had stopped half way. They were led astray by dreams of justice; their excessive magnanimity had prevented them from destroying the class enemy through ruthless extermination, and so they themselves had been massacred. The Soviet Union claimed to have succeeded where the Communards had failed. As a symbolic gesture, Lenin's body was wrapped in a red Federe flag.

Recently, historians have broken away from the Marxist interpretation, stressing the specifically French, republican and Parisian nature of the Commune. "It was," writes Jacques Rougerie, "the end of an era, dusk not dawn." Francois Furet concludes that "in this Paris in flames, the French Revolution bade farewell to history." However, some historians and sociologists, especially in America and Britain, have suggested that in other ways, as a specifically urban revolution, or in certain of its cultural aspects, or through the participation of women, the Commune can be seen as dawn as well as dusk. The debate will certainly continue.

The Siege of Paris Gives Rise to the First
Proletariat Government: 1871

The Lessons of the Paris Commune

by Alexander Tracutenberg

The Paris Commune and the provisional government that followed was the first revolution in which the working class played a central role and sought to change society for the better. Taken from a political pamphlet published in 1934, this essay acknowledges the sixtieth anniversary of the Paris Commune and describes why it was important to the labor movement and to the rise of European socialism following the commune. Even though the commune ultimately failed, the working-class government ruled Paris for seventy-two days and was the first proletariat dictatorship in history. What followed was one of the bloodiest conflicts in French history.

The years following the Paris Commune gave rise to more revolutionary activity throughout Europe and Russia. One of the most significant rebellions was the Russian Revolution in 1917, which led to the overthrow of the Russian czar and established a Socialist government for the first time in Europe. The Paris Commune inspired many of the principles espoused by the Russian revolutionaries. The revolutionaries and the Communards both believed that they were fighting a war of freedom from slave wages against an oppressive ruling class, and both were committed to ending the worldwide exploitation of laborers and craftsmen of all kinds. It became a momentous political movement across the world that still has momentum today.

Alexander Tracutenberg was a member of a Communist organization in New York called the John Reed Club. Named after muckraking journalist and radical John Reed, this short-lived club was

Alexander Tracutenberg, *The Lessons of the Paris Commune*. New York: International Pamphlets No. 12, 1934.

aligned with the Communist Party USA and was intended primarily to foster young leftist talent. Tracutenberg wrote several pamphlets for the club; in this pamphlet, he writes about the significance of the rise of the Paris Commune and why it was an event that had a major impact on the world.

On March 18, 1871, the revolutionary workers of Paris established the Commune. It was the first attempt at a proletarian dictatorship. Again and again the story has been told: how Napoleon III (the Little) attempted to bolster up the decaying regime of the Second Empire by declaring war on Prussia in July, 1871; how he met his debacle at Sedan and exposed Paris to the Prussian troops; how a bourgeois republic was proclaimed in September and a so-called Government of National Defense organized; how this Government betrayed the besieged city and how the Parisian masses rose and armed themselves for its defense; how they proclaimed the Commune on March 18, when the Government attempted to disarm their National Guard, and how they took the government of the city into their own hands; how the traitorous [Louis-Adolphe] Thiers Government withdrew to Versailles and there plotted with the Prussians the overthrow of the Commune; and how the Parisian workers held the Commune for seventy-two days, defending it to the last drop of blood when the Versailles troops had entered the city and slaughtered tens of thousands of the men and women who dared to seize the government of the capital and run it for the benefit of the exploited and disinherited.

Wherever workers will gather to hear once more the story of this heroic struggle—a story that has long since become a treasure of proletarian lore—they will honor the memory of the martyrs of 1871. But they will also remember those martyrs of the class struggle of today who have either been slaughtered or still smart in the dungeons of capitalist and colonial countries, for daring to rise against their oppressors—as the Parisian workers did sixty odd years ago.

The Battlefront Is Far-Flung

The Paris Commune lasted only 72 days, but it had a great many victims. More than 100,000 men and women were killed or exiled to the colonies when the bourgeoisie triumphed. Today the revolutionary battlefront is spread over a greater territory. It encircles almost the entire globe. Fierce class struggles are being fought in all capitalist and colonial countries; and tens of thousands of workers and peasants are killed or imprisoned. The total number of victims of fascism, the white terror and police brutality during the past years runs into many hundreds of thousands. Workers everywhere are rising to the defense of these victims of capitalist class justice, and the anniversary of the Commune calls especial attention to this important class duty of the workers. In the United States the workers are rallying to the banner of the International Labor Defense, which leads their struggle against every means of capitalist persecution. It fights for the right to strike and picket and against persecutions arising from all workers' struggles; it fights lynching and social and political discrimination against Negroes; it fights against the deportation of foreign-born workers and for the victims of every type of capitalist oppression and persecution.

The struggle for power, limited to a single city in 1871, has since become worldwide. One-sixth of the world already has been wrested from capitalist rule, and a Workers' Commune has been in power for more years than that of Paris lasted in weeks. In the Soviet Union the workers not only have defeated the bourgeoisie and beaten off the foreign invaders who came to its aid, but have so firmly established themselves that they already have begun to build the Socialist society of which the Paris Commune was a "glorious harbinger."

War Threatens the Soviet Union

But in the rest of the world—in the advanced capitalist countries and the backward colonies—the irrepressible conflict is day-by-day assuming greater proportions and a deeper meaning. The continued existence of workers' rule in what was once the Russian Empire and the great strides toward building Socialism there—a constant inspiration and guide post to the workers and peasants suffering under imperialist rule—drives the capitalist governments to plot the overthrow of the Soviet Union by organizing counter-revolution among the bourgeois remnants in the country, or war against it. The rivalries between imperialist powers will no more stop this drive for war in which the existence of a workers' government is at stake, than the rivalry between the French and Prussian bourgeoisie of 1811 could divide them when their community of interest demanded the defeat of the Paris Commune. The trials of the Industrial and Menshevik Parties have completely proved the conspiracies of the capitalist governments and the Second International against the Soviet Union through counter-revolutionary propaganda and acts of sabotage by their agents within the country. Continuous war provocations during recent years in the Far East, the erection of a vassal buffer state in Manchuria by Japan with the connivance of other imperialist powers, notwithstanding their conflicting interests in looting China, follows the policy of counter-revolutionary encirclement and war preparations against the Soviet Union and the annihilation of the Soviets established by the Chinese workers and peasants.

In commemorating the Paris Commune of 1871 the workers everywhere will bear in mind this constant war danger that hangs over the Soviet Commune of today; and they will organize for its defense. The Paris Commune suffered in part because it was isolated from other industrial centers and from the village districts, and because the international labor movement was then still too weak to be of material assistance to it. That is not true today. The Soviet Union has become an integral part of the revolutionary labor movement in all capitalist countries, and of the national liberation movements in the colonies. The working masses will leap to its defense and fight for it because they recognize that it is a part of their own struggle against capitalism and imperialism.

Workers Study the Lessons of the Commune

But the workers will not only draw inspiration from the heroic deeds of the Communards, who were "ready to storm the heavens" ([German political philosopher Karl] Marx). They will review the story of the Commune in the light of its achievements as well as of the errors and shortcomings for which the Parisian workers paid so dearly.

The absence of a disciplined, well-knit revolutionary leadership both prior to and after the establishment of the Commune spelled disaster at the outset. There was no unified and theoretically sound working class political party to put itself at the head of this elemental rising of the masses. Several groups competed for leadership—the Prudhonists, the Blanquists and the Internationalists were the most representative of them. And this doomed the Commune to continued confusion and indecision, to a lack of planning and of a long-range program. Piecemeal, day-to-day treatment of a rapidly developing revolutionary situation with utter neglect of tactics seemed to have been the practice of the leaders. Even the limited authority of the first days of the uprising was relinquished. As Marx noted in the celebrated letter to his friend Kugelman, written on April 12, 1871, "the Central Committee [of the National Guard] relinquished its powers too soon to pass them on to the Commune."

Revolutionary Fervor

Marx, the centralist, realized that a successful revolutionary struggle against Thiers' government could have been carried out by the Paris workers only under the leadership of a centralized revolutionary authority with military resources at its command. This authority was the Central Committee of the National Guard, but by renouncing its powers and turning its authority over to the loosely organized Commune, it dissipated the revolutionary energy of its armed forces. Yet, even while he analyzed the weaknesses of the Commune Marx showed an unbounded enthusiasm for the revolutionary fervor of the Communards. In the letter to Kugelman from which we already have quoted, and which was written three weeks after the proclaiming of the Commune, he grew almost rhapsodic. "What dexterity," he wrote, "what historical initiative, what ability for self-sacrifice these Parisians display. After six months of starvation and destruction, caused more by internal treachery than by the foreign enemy, they rise under Prussian bayonets as though there were no war between France and Germany, as if the enemy were not at the gates of Paris. History records no such example of heroism." He immediately followed this up, however, with a criticism of an error which was one of the costliest of the Commune: "If they are to be defeated it will be because of their 'magnanimity.' They should immediately have marched on Versailles, as soon as Viny and the reactionary portion of the National Guard escaped from Paris. The opportune moment was missed on account of 'conscientiousness.' They did not want to start a civil war—as if the monstrosity Thiers had not already begun it with his attempt to disarm Paris."

Marx, the revolutionary strategist, knew that when the enemy of revolutionary Paris was on the run, it was the job of the National Guard to pursue Thiers' defeated army and annihilate it, rather than to allow it time to reorganize its forces and return to fight the Paris workers. The "magnanimity" of the leaders of the Commune which Marx criticized led them to allow the ministers of the Thiers government and its reactionary supporters to depart to Versailles in peace, there to reorganize their forces and conspire against the Commune: it kept them from taking hostages from among the prominent bourgeois leaders who remained in the city and who took the opportunity to act as spies and form centers of counter-revolutionary activity. Had the Commune disarmed those troops which were under the influence of the reactionary government and held them in the city, they could have won over a great part of them, and neutralized others. Instead they were permitted to leave freely for Versailles, and to remain there under the continued tutelage of the reactionary militarists.

After the capture of power comes the immediate task of holding it and using it to spread and deepen the revolutionary struggle. When the Russian workers seized power in October, 1917, they did not rest there. Having learned from the mistakes of the Commune, the Russian Bolsheviks led the workers to a further offensive, not to end until every vestige of the old order had been uprooted and destroyed in the entire country and the working class firmly entrenched.

The Commune Fights for Power

The Commune was a struggle for power on the part of the working class. It was not merely a change of administration that the Paris workers saw in the development of the struggle. The clearest among the leaders, the followers of the International, knew that the conflict was assuming the proportions of a social revolution, although they, as well as the others, failed to work out the tactics necessary for the direction of the struggle. In another letter to Kugelman (April 17) Marx gave his interpretation in the following words: "The struggle of the capitalist class and its State machine has, thanks to the Paris Commune, entered a new phase. However it may end, a new landmark of international significance has been achieved."

This was precisely [Russian Communist leader Vladimir] Lenin's attitude regarding the December uprising in Moscow in 1905. The revolutionists of Moscow, who had the support of the masses, had either to accept the provocation of the Tsar's troops or go down in moral defeat before the Moscow workers. Though defeated, the revolutionists came out of that unequal struggle glorified by the entire working class of Russia. While the panicky Mensheviks were muttering the [George V.] Plekhanov formula, "They should not have resorted to arms," Lenin saw in the heroic struggle of the Moscow workers the revolutionary will to conquer of the Russian working class. Commenting on Marx's observation that the Paris workers had to take up the fight, Lenin wrote: "Marx could appreciate that there were moments in history when a struggle of the masses, even in a hopeless cause, was necessary for the sake of the future education of these masses and their training for the next struggle." It was this hopeful view of the Paris uprising applied to the revolutionary struggle of 1905 that led Lenin to maintain in 1907 in his introduction to the Kugelman letters: "The working class of Russia has already demonstrated once and will prove again that it is able to 'storm the heavens.'" And in 1917 it did.

The Bureaucracy Must Be Destroyed

The decrees of the Commune separating the church from the State confiscating church property, taking over the deserted factories, abolishing the payment of fines levied upon workers, prohibiting night work in bakeshops, etc., were all acts of great social import. These were the acts of a workers' government legislating in the interest of the working class. But the Commune did not take over all the factories. It did not take over the Bank of France. Instead, it went there to borrow (sic!) money for its revolutionary needs. Although the Commune seized the powers of the State, it tried to operate within the framework of the old State apparatus. Marx warned against this when, in his April 1 letter, he wrote of "the destruction of the bureaucratic political machine" as a prerequisite for a proletarian revolution. In his classic study of the Commune, *The Civil War in France*, an address read to the General Council of the First International two days after the fall of the Commune, he devoted a good deal of attention to the subject, and formulated this theoretical conclusion: "The working class cannot simply lay hold of the ready-made State machinery and wield it for its own purpose."

In 1891, the 20th anniversary of the Commune, [German Socialist Friedrich] Engels wrote an introduction to a new German edition of *The Civil War in France*. In criticizing the Commune for not taking over the Bank of France and using it for its own advantage, Engels points out that the Commune tried to utilize the old government apparatus. He comes back to what Marx took up in his "Address" by asserting that "the Commune should have recognized that the workers, having assumed power, cannot rule with the old State power, the machinery used before for its own exploitation," Engels concludes: "In truth, the State is nothing but an apparatus for the oppression of one class by another, in a democratic republic not less than in a monarchy."

The First Proletarian Revolution

Many are the lessons which the Commune has bequeathed to the international working class. Marx, Engels, and Lenin have studied the Commune closely, and the Russian workers showed that they mastered the lessons of the first proletarian revolution.

The Commune is the great tradition of the French working class. The mute walls of Père Lachaise [cemetery, where numerous Communards were executed] remind the French workers of the heroism of their proletarian fathers who fought for freedom from wage slavery. The Commune is also the heritage of the entire proletariat. It was the first revolution in which workers not only fought but which they also controlled and directed towards proletarian aims.

Writing on the 40th anniversary of the Commune, Lenin said: "In modern society the proletariat, enslaved by capital economically, cannot rule politically before breaking the chains which bind it to capital. This is why the Commune had to develop along socialist lines, that is, to attempt to overthrow the rule of the bourgeoisie, the rule of capital, the destruction of the very foundations of the present social order."

The Commune was the first attempt at proletarian dictatorship. It was not victorious but it was the prototype of the successful dictatorship inaugurated by the Russian workers forty-six years afterwards. Engels closes his introduction to *The Civil War in France*, quoted above, with the following passage: "The German philistine (read 'Socialist'—A.T.) has recently been possessed of a wholesome fear for the phrase: 'dictatorship of the proletariat.' Well then, gentlemen, do you want to know what this dictatorship is like? Look at the Paris Commune! This was the dictatorship of the proletariat!"

The Soviet, introduce in 1905 as a new form of representative working-class organization and firmly established in 1917 as a proletarian form of government, is of a higher type than the Paris Commune, and, according to Lenin, "the only form capable of insuring the least painful transition to Socialism." Lenin maintains, nevertheless, that this new state apparatus can be traced directly to the Commune. He speaks of the Soviet government "standing on the shoulders of the Paris Commune," that it is a "continuation of the Paris Commune," and that the Communist Party should state in its program that it strives "for Soviet power, for the Soviet type of government, for a government of the type of the Paris Commune."

The Great Soviet Commune was established by the Russian workers in 1917 under more favorable objective conditions, with a strongly welded revolutionary proletarian party to lead them, which the Parisian workers did not possess. Soviet Communes have also been established in China in the midst of the imperialist-ridden Far East—all direct lineal descendants of the short-lived proletarian dictatorship of 1871.

The Paris Commune is an epoch-making achievement of the revolutionary working class. Marx's tribute at the close of his historic "Address" testifies to the fealty of the world's proletariat to the memory of the valiant Communards and to the cause in behalf of which they fought: "Workingmen's Paris, with its Commune, will be forever celebrated as the glorious harbinger of the new society. Its martyrs are enshrined in the great heart of the working class. Its exterminators history has already nailed to that pillory from which all the prayers of their priests will not avail to redeem them."

And forty years afterward, in 1911, Lenin concluded an article on the anniversary of the Commune with the following trenchant words: "The cause of the Commune is the cause of the social revolution, the cause of the complete political and economic emancipation of the workers. It is the cause of the proletariat of the whole world. And in this sense it is immortal."

Impressionism Changed the Face of Art

by Otto Friedrich

Painter Claude Monet (1840–1926) was among a number of artists in Paris who developed an artistic style called impressionism. Together, the impressionists organized their own exhibition in 1874. Rebelling against the rigid and antiquated system of the French Academy at the close of the nineteenth century, masters such as Claude Monet, Édouard Manet, Camille Pissarro, Paul Cézanne, Berthe Morisot, Alfred Sisley, and Pierre-Auguste Renoir attempted to capture the fleeting effects of light and atmosphere of a single moment. The title of one of Monet's paintings, *Impression, Sunrise*, prompted the journalist Louis Leroy to dub the whole group of artists "impressionists," and the name, coined in derision, was later accepted by the artists themselves.

Impressionism is characterized by the use of a bright palette, broken brushwork, and an emphasis on the depictions of contemporary life and landscape. The impressionist artists worked with a simple and relatively loose set of rules. For example, paintings were supposed to be completed in a single session and never reworked. Pure black, pure white, and earth colors were not used. Taken directly from nature and the outside world, what landed on the canvas during the session remained. The result was a loose, fleeting, and dreamy effect. This disturbed the classical painters because it was antithetical to their academic and structured approach of mimicking reality. A closer examination of impressionist paintings, however, reveals that the works were hardly fleeting impressions but were based on logic, structure, and calculation.

The impressionists' efforts mirrored a period of dramatic change in society. The advancements in the Industrial Revolution brought improvements in technology, chemistry, and manufacturing. Art supplies were improved and updated, and the results were evident in the work of the impressionist painters.

Former editor of the *Saturday Evening Post* and winner of the George Polk Award in journalism, Otto Friedrich has published many articles and several books, including *A Portrait of Berlin in the 1920s*. In the following essay Friedrich describes how the impressionist exhibit of 1874 came to pass and how it marked a turning point in art history. He discusses the art, the exhibit, the artists, and how they survived in the society that initially rejected their work.

J ust as [composer Ludwig van] Beethoven didn't know that he had written the "Moonlight" Sonata until a minor critic named Rellstab bestowed its name upon it, just as [novelist Émile] Zola didn't know that he had written "*J'Accuse*" until the editor of *L'Aurore* put that headline on the diatribe that Zola had called "Letter to M. Felix Fauré, President of the Republic," so the impressionists didn't know that they were the Impressionists. They modestly announced that their show represented the Société Anonyme des Artistes, Peintres, Sculpteurs, Graveurs, etc.

The word had actually been in use for about ten years, notably by [Édouard] Manet, who had said at the time of his solo exhibition in 1867 that his goal was "to convey his impression." "Critics occasionally applied the term to the landscapes of [painters Jean-Baptiste-Camille] Corot, [Johan] Jongkind and [Charles-François] Daubigny, and one of them specifically praised Manet for his skill in capturing "the first impression of nature," but the full significance of the term emerged only from the storms that surrounded the exhibition of 1874. The catalogue was late, as usual, and there were arguments about the titles of various pictures. [Pierre-Auguste] Renoir's brother Edmond, who was trying to edit the catalogue, complained that [Claude] Monet's landscapes all seemed to have similar designations, *Morning in a Village, Evening in a Village*. . . . Monet himself later recalled that the dispute centered on a misty view of the harbor of Le Havre. "I couldn't very well call it a view of Le Havre. So I said: 'Put *Impression.*'" The picture actually was listed as *Impression, Sunrise.* It was only one of 165 pictures by thirty artists—among them [Edgar] Degas, Monet, Renoir, [Camille] Pissarro, [Paul] Cézanne, [Alfred] Sisley, and Berthe Morisot, but not Manet—but it inspired the malicious hostility of the critic Louis Leroy in the satirical magazine *Charivari,* who entitled his review "Exhibition of the Impressionists."

The Impression Is There

Leroy took with him to the exhibition an academic landscape painter named Joseph Vincent, winner of various official medals and prizes, and he wrote his review as a kind of mocking dialogue between the indignant voice of scholastic authority and himself as the innocently inquiring interviewer. Vincent's first shock came on seeing the beautiful Degas *Dancer* that is now in Washington's National Gallery of Art. "What a pity," said Vincent, "that the painter, who has a certain understanding of color, doesn't draw better; his dancer's legs are as cottony as the gauze of her skirts." Next came Pissarro's *Ploughed Field:* "Those furrows? . . . But they are palette scrapings placed uniformly on a dirty canvas. It has neither head nor tail, top nor bottom, front nor back."

"Perhaps . . . but the impression is there," Leroy offered.

"Well, it's a funny impression!" snapped Vincent.

Then came Monet's marvelous scene of crowds strolling on the snowy Boulevard des Capucines. "'Ah-hah!' he sneered. . . . 'Is that brilliant enough, now! There's impression, or I don't know what it means. Only be so good as to tell me what those innumerable black tongue-lickings in the lower part of the picture represent?'

"'Why, those are people walking along,' I replied.

"'Then do I look like that when I'm walking along the Boulevard des Capucines? Blood and thunder! So you're making fun of me at last!'"

And then, inevitably, the two nay-sayers arrived in front of Berthe Morisot's exquisite portrait of Edma admiring her new baby in *The Cradle.* Vincent was outraged by the delicate image of Edma's hand on the cradle. "Now take Mlle. Morisot," he protested. "That young lady is not interested in producing trifling details. When she has a hand to paint, she makes exactly as many brushstrokes lengthwise as there are fingers, and the business is done. Stupid people who are finicky about the drawing of a hand don't understand a thing about impressionism, and the great Manet would chase them out of his republic."

Leroy had been so unerringly accurate in singling out the most gifted of his contemporaries to be excoriated as "Impressionists" that the painters of the "Société Anonyme des Artistes" could hardly help accepting their new name. Like the "wild beasts" who later took pride in having been denounced as "*les fauves*," the impressionists remained the Impressionists.

An Unfashionable Practice

They did not suddenly appear out of nowhere as a "school," of course. As often happens when the younger generation suddenly becomes famous, they were already approaching middle age at the time of their first exhibition in 1874. Monet, Cézanne, Renoir, and Berthe Morisot were all in their mid-thirties, Degas already forty, Pissarro forty-four (and Manet forty-two). But this emergence of the Impressionist group had been more than a decade in the coming. These young painters had been attracted from all over to the booming imperial Paris of the early 1860s. Claude Monet, for one, was the son of a prosperous grocer in Le Havre. He ignored his schoolwork, doodled in his notebooks, and soon became locally celebrated as a caricaturist. He inevitably encountered another local celebrity, Eugène Boudin, who devoted himself to the very unfashionable practice of painting seascapes, which the seventeen-year-old Monet regarded "with an intense aversion." Boudin was not to be discouraged, however. "Boudin, with untiring kindness, undertook my education," Monet later recalled. "My eyes were finally opened and I really understood nature; I learned at the same time to love it." Boudin urged the young apprentice onward to Paris, and so, with the reluctant approval of his parents, Monet headed for the capital. He refused to enroll in the stodgy École des Beaux Arts, however preferring a simpler institution known as the Académie Suisse, where artists could paint live models or work at whatever they liked, without any examinations. Monet's father promptly cut off his allowance.

Monet soon met a fellow student named Camille Pissarro, son of a storekeeper on the Caribbean island of St. Thomas, who had run away from home to become a painter. The two youths struck up a friendship and went out on painting expeditions together.

That camaraderie was interrupted by Monet's being summoned to seven years' conscription in the army. His father offered to buy a substitute, as was common in those days; Monet refused. "The seven years of service that appalled so many were full of attraction to me . . ." he said. "In Algeria I spent two really charming years. I incessantly saw something new; in my moments of leisure I attempted to render what I saw. You cannot imagine to what extent I increased my knowledge, and how much my vision gained thereby. I did not quite realize it at first. The impressions of light and color that I received there were not to classify themselves until later; they contained the germ of my future researches."

Returning to Paris

Monet fell ill in Algeria, however, so he had to accede to his father's paying for his discharge. He returned to Paris early in 1862—by now bushy-haired and thickly bearded—and compromised with his father's desire for some professional discipline by enrolling in the studio of Charles Gleyre. An eminent conservative, Gleyre was nonetheless a relatively easygoing teacher whose other pupils included the young Renoir, [James] Whistler, Sisley, and [Jean-Frédéric] Bazille.

They were all, to some extent, Gleyre's black sheep. "The first week I worked there most conscientiously," Monet later recalled, "and made, with as much application as spirit, a study of the nude from the living model. . . . The following week, when he [Gleyre] came to me, he sat down and, solidly planted in my chair, looked attentively at my production. Then he turned round and, leaning his grave head to one side with a satisfied air, said to me: 'Not bad! not bad at all, that thing there, but it is too much in the character of the model—you have before you a short thick-set man, you paint him short and thick-set—he has enormous feet, you render them as they are. All that is very ugly. I want you to remember, young man, that when one draws a figure, one should always think of the antique. Nature, my friend, is all right as an element of study, but it offers no interest. Style, you see, is everything.'"

Renoir had similar problems. One of five children of a tailor in Limoges, he had started as an apprentice painter of the local porcelain, but he too, now twenty-one, had arrived in Paris in that same year of 1862 to fulfill a higher ambition. He too had copied the model as realistically as he could.

"No doubt it's to amuse yourself that you are dabbling in

paint?" inquired the lordly teacher.

"Why, of course," said the ebullient young Renoir, "and if it didn't amuse me, I beg you to believe that I wouldn't do it!"

The Artists Meet

It is strange and striking how the great composers of the early nineteenth century—[Frédéric-François] Chopin, [Franz] Liszt, [Robert] Schumann, [Hector] Berlioz, [Richard] Wagner—all recognized each other instantly when they were still in their early twenties. Much the same thing happened among the future Impressionists. Monet was still only twenty-two when he met the twenty-one-year-old Renoir at Gleyre's studio and they began going off to paint landscapes together. Cézanne, the schoolmate of Zola, had met Pissarro the previous year, and Pissarro already knew Monet. Manet and Degas met while copying in the Louvre, and [Henri] Fantin-Latour introduced Berthe Morisot to Monet there. Most of these painters (not, of course, the ultra-respectable Berthe Morisot) met regularly at the Café de Guerbois, a small and relatively quiet establishment on the Grande Rue des Batignolles (now the Avenue de Clichy), and so the group came to be known as the Batignolles group. When Fantin-Latour painted his splendidly documentary *Studio in the Batignolles Quarter* (1870), he placed Manet before an easel in the center, then surrounded him with such younger admirers as Monet, Renoir, Bazille, and Zola.

The goal of the young painters' training was a showing at the official Salon, but as the students observed the Salon jurors' treatment of Manet, whose work they much admired, they began to think about alternative courses. The year after Monet and Renoir first encountered each other at Gleyre's studio was the year when they saw the Salon jurors reject *Le Déjeuner sur l'herbe* and *Mlle. V . . . in the Costume of an Espada*, and saw both these paintings of Mlle. Victorine Meurent appear before the mocking visitors to the Salon des Refusés. An even more important breaking point came four years later when both Manet and [Jean] Courbet decided separately not to submit anything to the Salon but to build separate pavilions and exhibit their works to visitors to the World's Fair of 1867. After both these private exhibitions closed, both failures in any critical or commercial sense, Courbet hoped to rent out the pavilion he had built, and Monet and his friends hoped to move into it.

"I shan't send anything more to the jury," Bazille wrote to his family. "It is far too ridiculous . . . to be exposed to these administrative whims. . . . What I say here, a dozen young people of talent think along with me. We have therefore decided to rent each year a large studio where we'll exhibit as many of our works as we wish. We shall invite painters whom we like to send pictures. . . . Many others whom you perhaps do not know, have promised to send us pictures and very much approve of our idea. With these people, and Monet, who is stronger than all of them, we are sure to succeed. . . ." But that time was not yet. Bazille soon wrote again to his family: "I spoke to you of the plan some young people had of making a separate exhibition. Bleeding ourselves as much as possible, we were able to collect the sum of 2,500 francs, which is not sufficient. We are therefore obliged to give up what we wanted to do."

Artists in Poverty

Poverty affects the history of art as much as wealth. Just as Manet and Degas and Berthe Morisot could pursue their experiments without any worries about the next meal, some of the younger painters were severely handicapped by their penury. Renoir was so penniless during the unsuccessful 1867 fundraising that he had to beg a friend to provide the canvas so that he could paint a portrait of the friend's sister-in-law. The following year, both Renoir and Pissarro were reduced to painting window blinds in order to survive. Perhaps the most afflicted of all was Monet, who had started in 1866 what he called "experimenting with effects of light and color." One of these experiments was to dig a trench in his garden near Saint-Cloud so that he could undertake a large painting entirely out of doors. The following year, he began his first cityscapes. But all through this period, his letters to various friends and acquaintances contain repeated appeals for money. Thus to Bazille, who had a modest allowance, in 1868: "I am writing you a few lines in haste to ask your speedy help. I was certainly born under an unlucky star. I have just been thrown out of the inn, and stark naked at that. My family have no intention of doing anything more for me. I don't even know where I'll have a place to sleep tomorrow. . . . I was so upset yesterday that I had the stupidity to throw myself into the water. Fortunately, no harm came of it."

Monet's finances were never munch better than disastrous, but now they became worse than before because he had become involved with a nineteen-year-old girl named Camille Doncieux. She was not a great beauty but handsome, and a personality of considerable patience and character, as anyone would have to be to survive life with Monet. Just a few days after he met her, he quickly painted a full-length portrait for the Salon of 1866. It attracted considerable attention, for it is a remarkable portrait, the face barely visible, turned away to one side, the eyes closed, so that Monet the colorist could devote great attention to his beloved's flowing green-striped dress. He then had her pose—again with her dress, this time white-flowered, more important than her face—for a huge (eight-foot-high) painting called *Women in the Garden.* The practical problem was that Camille was now pregnant, and Monet could not even support himself, much less a family. Out of a mixture of admiration and charity, Bazille bought *Women in the Garden* on the installment plan, fifty francs a month. Monet then fled from the Paris suburb of Ville d'Avray to his native Le Havre to escape his creditors. In an effort to hide his unsold paintings from the creditors, he slit some 200 canvases from their frames and stored them away; the creditors found them and sold them off at the now-incredible price of thirty francs for each lot of fifty paintings.

Begging for Help

Monet's only recourse was to beg his father for help, but he could not bring himself to that final humiliation. So it was Bazille who wrote the letter, describing not only Monet's poverty but explaining that his first child was soon to be born. The elder Monet's answer was chilling. He said that he had a sister living in the Le Havre suburb of Saint-Adresse, who would be kind enough to offer her scapegrace nephew his room and board, but no money. As for the pregnant Camille, the elder Monet disapproved of her and showed no interest in his prospective grandchild. He said that young Claude should abandon them both.

And Monet did. He went to live with his aunt, leaving Camille in Paris without a sou. The baby was born that July of 1867 and named Jean. Monet claimed that he could not raise the train fare to visit them. Later that summer, while working at his easel alongside Sisley at Honfleur, Monet mysteriously suffered a temporary blindness. Cézanne once said that Monet was "nothing but an eye, but what an eye," and we are too far away in space and time to do more than wonder at the frequency with which these Impressionist painters, so obsessed with their visions of light and color, suffered serious eye trouble. Degas spent much of his life struggling with a progressive blindness that finally forced him to shift from painting to sculpture. His highly gifted protégé Mary Cassatt endured the last ten years of her life blind. Renoir, Pissarro, Cézanne, they all saw their vision falter and fail. Monet, too, went blind near the end but was saved by a delicate eye operation.

He somehow recovered from this early crisis and got himself back to Paris, where he and Renoir shared Bazille's studio on the Rue Visconti. "Monet has fallen upon me from the skies with a collection of magnificent canvases," the ever-generous Bazille wrote to his sisters. And Camille took him back, so Monet painted a charming picture of her presiding over the young Jean's cradle. And the struggle went on. "My painting doesn't go, and I definitely do not count any more on fame," Monet wrote to Bazille in 1868. "I'm getting very sunk. . . . As soon as I make up my mind to work, I see everything black. In addition, money is always lacking. Disappointments, insults, hopes, new disappointments. . . ." At least Camille believed in him. They were finally married in June of 1870, less than two months before the war against Prussia suddenly broke out.

Bound by Deep Beliefs

They were remarkably different people, these young impressionists—Monet the passionate visionary. Renoir the carefree hedonist, Pissarro the idealistic socialist, Berthe Morisot the acerbic aristocrat—and yet they were bound together by their deep belief in a series of radical propositions. One was the conviction commonly herd by ambitious young artists, that the gates of the establishment must be broken open. Let the new generation be heard. Another, more important, was that the tradition of historical painting must give way to scenes of contemporary life, *la vie moderne.* And that the tradition of studio composition must give way to a new process of painting out of doors, *en plein air.* And that a painting need not be "finished," in the sense that every detail must be fully shown by nearly invisible brushwork. "The grand manner and subject painting began to go obviously out of date," [Paul] Valéry wrote. "Filling the walls left bare of Greeks, Turks, Knights, and Cupids, landscape came and demolished the problems of *subject*, and in a few years reduced the whole intellectual side of art to a few questions about *materials* and the coloring of shadows. The brain became nothing but retina; there could no longer be any question of trying to express in paint the feelings of a group of old men before a beautiful Susanna. . . ."

In that phrase about "the coloring of shadows," Valéry merely suggests what is perhaps the most important innovation among the Impressionists, a new sense of light and of how to convey light in pictures. In his authoritative *History of Impressionism*, John Rewald offers a succinct analysis: "Manet liked to maintain that for him 'light appeared with such unity that a single tone was sufficient to convey it and that it was preferable, even though apparently crude, to move abruptly from light to shadow than to accumulate things which the eye doesn't see and which not only weaken the strength of the light but enfeeble the color scheme of the shadows, which it is important to concentrate on.' But those among Manet's companions who had already worked out-of-doors, that is, all the landscapists in the group, must have objected to his manner of dividing a subject merely into lighted and shadowed areas. Their experience with nature had taught them otherwise. Little by little they were abandoning the usual method of suggesting the third dimension by letting the so-called local color of each object become more somber as the object itself seemed further away from the source of light and deeper in the shadow. Their own observations had taught them that the parts in the shadow were not devoid of color nor merely darker than the rest. Being to a lesser degree penetrated by the light, the shaded areas did not, of course, show the same color values as those exposed to the sun, but they were just as rich in color, among which complimentaries and especially blue seemed to dominate. By observing and reproducing these colors, it became possible to indicate depth without resorting to any of the bitumens customarily reserved for shadows. At the same time the general aspect of the work became automatically brighter. In order to study these questions further Monet, Sisley, and Pissarro began to devote themselves especially to winter landscapes. . . ."

Nature's Colors

"White does not exist in nature," Renoir explained long afterward in examining a young student's snow scene. "You admit that you have a sky above that snow. Your sky is blue. That blue must show up in the snow. In the morning there is green and yellow in the sky. These colors also must show up in the snow when you say that you painted your picture in the morning. Had you done it in the evening red and yellow would have to appear in the snow. And look at the shadows. They are much too dark. That tree, for example, has the *same* local color on the side where the sun shines as on the side where the shadow is. But you paint it as if it were two different objects, one light and one dark. Yet the color of the object is the same, only with a veil thrown over it. Sometimes that veil is thin, sometimes thick, but always it remains a veil. . . . Shadows are not black; no shadow is black. It always has a color. Nature knows only colors. . . . White and black are not colors."

More generally, Pissarro told another young student, also many years later, how these perceptions of light should be applied: "Look for the kind of nature that suits your temperament. The motif should be observed more for shape and color than for drawing. . . . Do not define too closely the outline of things; it is the brush stroke of the right value and color which should produce the drawing. In a mass, the greatest difficulty is not to give the contour in detail, but to paint what is within. Paint the essential character of things, try to convey it by any means, without bothering about technique. . . . Don't work bit by bit, but paint everything at once by placing tones everywhere. . . . Use small brush strokes and try to put down your perceptions immediately. The eye should not be fixed on one point, but should take in everything, while observing the reflections which the colors produce on their surroundings. Work at the same time upon sky, water, branches, ground, keeping everything going on an equal basis and unceasingly rework until you have got it. Cover the canvas at the first go, then work at it until you can see nothing more to add. Observe the aerial perspective well, from the foreground to the horizon, the reflections of sky, of foliage. Don't be afraid of putting on color, refine the work little by little. Don't proceed according to rules and principles but paint what you observe and feel. Paint generously and unhesitatingly, for it is best not to lose the first impression. Don't be timid in front of nature; one must be bold, at the risk of being deceived and making mistakes."

Joining Forces

If the Impressionists' first effort to join forces in 1867 was thwarted by their poverty, their growing sense of community toward the end of the 1860s was shattered by the sudden outbreak of the Franco-Prussian War. While Manet and Degas joined the armed forces defending Paris, and Berthe Morisot remained in the besieged city, many painters were more interested in painting than in taking up arms for the dissolute emperor or his patchwork successors. Pissarro fled to London, leaving fifteen years' accumulated work behind him in Louveciennes. Monet, too, decided to go to London, once again leaving the indomitable Camille to fend for herself.

Monet and Pissarro soon found each other, through the good offices of the refugee art dealer Paul Durand-Ruel, the future sponsor of the whole Impressionist movement, who included new works by both of his new discoveries in a London exhibition of French artists. Monet and Pissarro then went off painting and museum-visiting together, just as though nothing were happening back in France. "The water colors and paintings of [Joseph] Turner and [John] Constable have certainly had influence upon us," Pissarro recalled. "We admired, [Thomas] Gainsborough, [Thomas] Lawrence, [Joshua] Reynolds, etc., but we were struck chiefly by the landscape painters, who shared more in our aim with regard to *plein air*, light, and fugitive effects. . . . Turner and Constable, while they taught us something, showed us in their works that they had no understanding of the *analysts of shadow*, which in Turner's painting is simply used as an effect, a mere absence of light. . . ."

For such disdain, Pissarro got his reward. "Here there is no art; everything is a question of business . . ." he wrote to a friend. "One gathers only contempt, indifference, even rudeness." And the owner of his house in Louveciennes wrote him that the Prussians had occupied the place and vandalized his paintings: "There are a few which these gentlemen, for fear of dirtying their feet, put on the ground in the garden to serve them as a carpet." All in all, Pissarro estimated, "about forty pictures are left to me out of 1,500." As for Monet, he returned from London only after a leisurely detour through Holland, then picked up the faithful Camille again, moved her to the riverside suburb of Argenteuil, and started painting new portraits of her. She was no longer the handsome girl of the prewar years. Posed next to a mass of bright red flowers in *Mme. Monet on a Garden Bench* (1872–73), she now has a mournful look in her dark-circled eyes.

Forget the Salon

The young Impressionists liked to go out in pairs—Monet and Renoir, Pissarro and Cézanne—and to paint the same scenes from the same vantage point, all learning from each other's gifts and perceptions. Yet the doors of the official Salon still remained largely closed to them. Renoir submitted two canvases for the Salon of 1873, and both were rejected; Monet, Pissarro, and Sisley didn't even bother to try. So the scene was set for one of Zola's friends, Paul Alexis, apparently prodded by the painters of the Café Guerbois. He published an article in *L'Avenir National* in May of 1873 calling on the young painters to forget about the Salon and organize a showing of their own works.

Monet immediately responded to the cue. "A group of painters assembled in my home has read with pleasure the article which you have published in *L'Avenir National*," he wrote to Alexis. "We are happy to see you defend ideas which are ours too, and we hope that, as you say, *L'Avenir National* will kindly give us assistance when the society which we are about to form will be completely constituted." Alexis in turn picked up Monet's cue, published his letter, and announced that "several artists of great merit"—including Pissarro, Sisley, and Jongkind—had already joined Monet's nascent "society." "These painters, most of whom have previously exhibited, belong to that group of naturalists which has the right ambition of painting nature and life in their large reality," Alexis wrote. "Their association, however, will not be just a small clique. They intend to represent interests, not tendencies, and hope for the adhesion of all serious artists."

As happens every time that some young people start a new movement appealing to "all serious artists," the first question was, who would pay the bills? A rich participant? Someone's mistress? A social-climbing merchant? One Person who could not pay was Durand-Ruel, the art dealer who had by now acquired the largest collection of the young painters' works. The postwar boom had ended abruptly in 1873, and Durand-Ruel had to cut back drastically on his investments. The most logical solution was for the painters to sponsor themselves, with each participant putting up an advance of sixty francs. Those who signed the founding charter on December 27, 1873, included Monet, Degas, Renoir, Pissarro, and Berthe Morisot. The main trouble with this system was that it gave everyone the right to argue about every detail.

Organizing the Exhibit

The most fundamental disagreement, which was to haunt the movement throughout its existence, was whether the exhibit should be large or small, and if it was to be limited, who should decide on the limits? This was the same problem that had plagued the Salon ever since the beginning, for the despised jury was there to make just such decisions. But the new movement rejected the whole idea of a jury; the painters were to make their own selections, of their own works, and therefore the founders had to decide which painters to admit. To such natural leaders as Monet and Pissarro, it seemed obvious that the exhibition should concentrate on the new tendencies, the new concern with landscapes and light. But Degas felt very strongly that the exhibition should not appear radical, not a movement, simply independent of the official system.

One thing that almost all of the founding members of the group agreed on was that they wanted to include Manet, their pioneering hero who had fought all the battles of the 1860s. They could hardly believe it when Manet repeatedly refused their invitations. But he was not really an Impressionist; he painted entirely in his studio, he had little interest in landscapes, and though he did engage in radical experiments with light and color, they were experiments all his own. No less important, Manet rejected the Impressionists precisely because they rejected the Salon. Always the reluctant revolutionary, Manet believed strongly that the Salon was the battlefield where the artistic wars could and should be fought. Independent exhibitions, as he knew all too well, amounted to very little in comparison to the Salon. And furthermore, he also believed—a recurrent delusion of his—that victory was finally in sight. At the Salon of 1873, he had won high praises for *Le bon Bock*, his rather conventional, comfortable portrait, in the manner of Franz Hals, of a bearded man contentedly sipping his beer and puffing his long pipe. Better yet, he had sold it for 6,000 francs, his highest price yet. For that matter, the watchful Durand-Ruel had come to visit his studio in 1872 and bought almost everything there—some two dozen paintings—for 49,000 francs.

"Why don't you stay with me?" Manet urged Monet and Renoir. "You can see very well that I am on the right track!" "Exhibit with us; you'll receive an honorable mention," he said to Degas. He strenuously urged the same views on Berthe Morisot, who stubbornly defied him, though Éva Gonzalès remained the loyal pupil. The Impressionists, for their part, continued the argument too. "Manet seems to become obstinate in his decision to remain apart; he may very well regret it . . . ." Degas wrote to a friend in London. "The realist movement . . . has to *show itself separately*. There has to *be a realist Salon*. Manet doesn't understand that. I definitely believe him to be much more vain than intelligent." That was unjust, but Manet was indeed difficult (through certainly no more so than Degas). Pissarro insisted that his temperamental friend Cézanne join the group, and Manet reacted by saying: "I'll never commit myself with M. Cézanne." And he probably did not yet know that one of Cézanne's three submissions to the new exhibition was *A Modern Olympia*, a slapdash burlesque of Manet's masterpiece. Degas, who wanted a broad variety of participants, kept arguing. To Félix Braquemond, the last of the thirty to join, he wrote: "We are gaining a famous recruit in you. Be assured of the pleasure and good you are doing us. (Manet, stirred up by Fantin-Latour and confused by himself, is still holding out, but nothing seems to be final in that direction.)"

They finally had a bitter confrontation, a few years later, about this continuing controversy. One of Degas's friends won the Legion of Honor, a decoration for which Manet hungered. Degas scorned it and him.

"All that contempt, my boy, is nonsense . . ." Manet said. "If there were no rewards, I wouldn't invent them; but they exist. . . . It is another weapon. In this beastly life of ours, which is wholly struggle, one is never too well armed. I haven't been decorated? But it is not my fault, and I assure you that I shall be if I can and that I shall do everything necessary to that end."

"Naturally," said Degas, the banker's son, "I've always known how much of a bourgeois you are."

Finding a Space

Somehow, the arguments did get settled. Pissarro, who had had experience in various Socialist enterprises, suggested a joint stock company, with each stockholder signing the official regulations. Each participant would give the group one-tenth of any sales. Manet's friend Nadar . . . loaned the group his studio, rent-free, on the second floor of a building at the corner of the Rue d'Aunou and the Boulevard des Capucines, just a bit south of the new opera house. That address inspired Degas, who was still try-

ing to avoid any suggestion of a rebellions new faction, to pro-
pose that the group adopt the neutral name of La Capucine (nas-
turtium); the others preferred the even more neutral name of Société Anonyme des Artistes, Peintres, Sculpteurs, Graveurs, etc.
As for the touchy question of how the assembled works should
be hung, Pissarro won approval for an elaborate system whereby
pictures would first be classified according to size and then
arranged by a drawing of lots.

The official opening took place on April 15, 1874—two weeks
before the official Salon, to make it clear that this was no collection of castoffs, no new Salon des Refusés. Looking back, we
can only marvel that such a magnificent collection of pictures
could be assembled, all new, in one time and place. Degas's *Car-
riage at the Races*, for example, in which the serene expanse of
a pale green meadow all comes into focus on a tiny baby being
fed under a while parasol, watched by a man in a top hat and a
large black dog. Or Renoir's *The Loge*, in which a handsome
woman in a black-and-white-striped dress, with a pink flower in
her red hair, gazes reflectively out at the theater audience while
her escort surveys the balcony through his binoculars. And from
Berthe Morisot not only the unforgettable *Cradle* but also the de-
licious *Hide and Seek*, a mother and her young daughter, both
fully outfitted in beribboned hats, pretending to find and be
found behind a transparent shrub.

The critics played their predictable roles as blind and ignorant
buffoons, with Leroy leading the way in *Charivari*. The con-
demnation and derision caused Madame Morisot to worry that
even though her difficult daughter was now at least engaged, her
association with such controversial artists might bring disgrace
upon the family. She asked Berthe's one-time teacher, Guichard,
that prophet who had warned that Berthe's determination to become a painter would be "a disaster," to visit the exhibition and
give her his judgment. "When I entered I became anguished
upon seeing the works of your daughter in those pernicious surroundings," Guichard wrote back. "I said to myself: 'One doesn't
live with impunity among madmen. Manet was right in opposing her participation.' After examining and analyzing conscientiously, one certainly finds here and there some excellent frag-
ments, but they all have more or less *cross-eyed minds.*"

If the first Impressionist exhibition had relatively little effect
on critics and other artists, it had even less on the public or the

market. The number of visitors on opening day amounted to only 175—and many of them came only to jeer—as compared to a daily average of nearly 10,000 at the Salon. All in all, some 3,500 came to the Impressionists' month-long exhibit, 400,000 to the Salon. A few Impressionist paintings were sold, but the sales receipts no longer record which ones, and the sums involved were derisory. Total sales figures, derived from the 10 percent commission collected by the group, amounted to only 3,600 francs. Sisley earned 1,000 francs, Monet 200, Renoir 180, Degas and Berthe Morisot nothing, and this at a time when a popular hack like Ernest Meissonier, Manet's commander during the war, charged 100,000 francs for a commissioned painting.

The exhibition seemed for a time to have broken even on its entrance fees, catalogue sales, and commissions, but at the end of the year, Renoir summoned all available stockholders to his studio on the Rue Saint-Georges and told them that they still owed 3,435 francs, or 184.50 apiece. He therefore proposed liquidating the Société Anonyme des Artistes, Peintres, Sculpteurs, Graveurs, etc., and his proposal was approved unanimously. So the first exhibition of the group now known as Impressionists (though Degas still adamantly rejected the term) both was a historic event and was not a historic event. It was an almost total failure, and yet it established a landmark, created a new sense of common dedication and commitment. But the real history of the Impressionist movement, with its rending conflicts and controversies, was yet to come.

Painting Light: An Interview with Claude Monet

by Francois Thiébault-Sisson

Early in his career, Claude Monet was well known in his native Paris for drawing and selling caricatures. Soon afterward he began to paint. After spending seven years in the army, he returned to Paris and two years later had his first public exhibit. At the time, the popular form of painting was classical and was most often completed in a studio. Monet and his friends did their work outdoors, in nature— a style referred to as *plein air*. Monet began studying color and light and painting in a way that affronted accepted customs. He influenced art by painting spontaneously, giving a personal response to outdoor scenes or events.

Like many famous artists and innovators, his work was initially rejected and met with consistent criticism. Nonetheless, he managed to find ways to show his work and continued painting in his own unique and personal style.

Several years after his first exhibit, Monet met and began painting with other young artists in Paris, including Edgar Degas, Paul Cézanne, Alfred Sisley, Jean-Frédéric Bazille, and Pierre-Auguste Renoir. The painters also kept company with early-career writers and art critics such as Émile Zola and the art critic Edmond Duranty. These artists and writers were interested in similar pursuits and were likewise marginalized by the Paris art scene. The artists formed their own guild so they could organize and show their work

---

Francois Thiébault-Sisson, "Claude Monet: An Interview," *Le Temps*, November 27, 1900.

together. Eventually, the group came to be known as the "impressionists." In the late 1870s some of the painters finally began to sell their work.

The following article was published in the Paris daily newspaper *Le Temps* (*The Times*) on November 27, 1900. Claude Monet was sixty years old and had already achieved a certain degree of world celebrity. In this interview with art critic Francois Thiébault-Sisson, Monet discusses his life and influences.

There has just been opened in Mr. [Paul] Durand-Ruel's Galleries, Rue Laffitte, an exhibition of from twenty-five to thirty-canvases by Claude Monet, in which a decided change of the artist's manner is noticed. Here we see the most varied aspects of natured reflected in pictures, both serene and striking in their breadth of interpretation. From the abrupt palisades of the Fjords or from the steep declivities of Norman cliffs, from the ravines in the valley of the Creuse, or from the dreamy banks of the Seine, from ponds peopled with waterlilies, or decked with the purple of the Iris, there emanates the same comprehensive impression, most unique and powerful in its synthetical qualities. The filmy transparency of mists and the subtlety of atmospheric effects spread over the vivacity of color, over the wildness or mildness of the subjects, a peaceful softness that acts as a charm, and the landscape thus treated becomes ennobled and rises to a singular loftiness.

All the elements of nature are transposed; they are metamorphosed into a personal interpretation, where naught is admitted but that which is expressive, into a comprehensive view, where alone the essential characters appear, and their re-union, dictated by selection, constitutes the most penetrating and the most real, the most poetical and the most moving of decorations.

Unless I am much mistaken, this exposition will be followed and studied with passionate interest, even by those who still argue against this rare and original talent.

Now is the time, it would seem, or never, to make known to the readers of *Le Temps* otherwise than by the review of his works, the master who has given to Impressionism its doctrine and who has furnished its most frank and fearless examples. He came out of his retreat at Giverny for one day. He gave himself the satisfaction of being present at the opening of his Exposition.

I met him there by chance, and in spite of his resistance, dragged him to my lair. There, fixing upon me his blue eyes, eyes which flash like those of a man of twenty, and stroking with one hand the silky waves of his long beard, where a few blond threads still linger in the snow with which three score years have sprinkled it, he briefly told me his history.

"I am a Parisian from Paris. I was born there in 1840, under good King Louis-Philippe, in a circle entirely given over to commerce, and where all professed a contemptuous disdain for the arts. But my youth was passed at Hâvre, where my father had settled in 1845, to follow his interests more closely, and this youth was essentially that of a vagabond. I was undisciplined by birth; never would I bend, even in my most tender youth, to a rule. It was at home that I learned the little I know. School always appeared to me like a prison, and I never could make up my mind to stay there, not even for four hours a day, when the sunshine was inviting, the sea smooth, and when it was such a joy to run about on the cliffs, in the free air, or to paddle around in the water."

A Wholesome Beginning

"Until I was fourteen or fifteen years old, I led this irregular but thoroughly wholesome life, to the despair of my poor father. Between times I had picked up in a hap-hazard way the rudiments of arithmetic and a smattering of orthography. This was the limit of my studies. They were not over tiresome for they were intermingled for me with distractions. I made wreaths on the margins of my books; I decorated the blue paper of my copy-books with ultra-fantastical ornaments, and I represented thereon, in the most irreverent fashion, deforming them as much as I could, the face or the profile of my masters.

"I soon acquired much skill at this game. At fifteen I was known all over Hâvre as a caricaturist. My reputation was so well established that I was sought after from all sides and asked for caricature-portraits. The abundance of orders and the insufficiency of the subsidies derived from maternal generosity inspired me with a bold resolve which naturally scandalized my family; I took money for my portraits. According to the appearance of my clients, I charged ten or twenty francs for each portrait, and the scheme worked beautifully. In a month my patrons had doubled in number. I was now able to charge twenty francs in all cases without lessening the number of orders. If I had kept on, I would to-day be a millionaire.

"Having gained consideration by these means, I was soon an important personage in the town. In the show-window of the only framemaker who was able to make his expenses in Hâvre my caricatures arrogantly displayed themselves five or six in a row, framed in gold and glazed, like highly artistic works, and when I saw the loungers crowd before them in admiration and heard them, pointing them out, say: 'That is so and so:' I nearly choked with vanity and self-satisfaction."

The First Teacher

"Still there was a shadow in all this glory. Often in the same show-window, I beheld, hung over my own productions, marines that I, like most of my fellow citizens, thought disgusting. And, at heart, I was much vexed to have to endure this contact, and never ceased to abuse the idiot, who, thinking he was an artist, had enough self-complacency to sign them,—this idiot was [French painter Eugène-Louis] Boudin. In my eyes, . . . the sincere little compositions of Boudin, with his little figures so true, his ships so accurately rigged, his skies and his water so exact, drawn and painted only from nature, these had nothing artistic, and their fidelity struck me as more than suspicious. Therefore his painting inspired me with an intense aversion, and without knowing the man I hated him. Often the framemaker would say to me: 'You should make the acquaintance of Mr. Boudin. You see, whatever they may say of him, he knows his trade. He studied it in Paris, in the studios of the *Ecole des Beaux-Arts*. He could give you some good advice.'

"And I resisted with silly pride. What indeed could such a ridiculous man teach me?

"Still the day came, fatal day, when chance brought me, in spite of myself, face to face with Boudin. He was in the rear of the shop, and not noticing his presence, I entered. The framemaker grasped the opportunity and without consulting me presented me: 'Just see, Mr. Boudin, this is the young man who has so much talent for caricature'—and Boudin, without hesitation, came to me, complimented me in his gentle voice and said: 'I always look at them with much pleasure, your sketches; they are amusing, clever, bright. You are gifted; one can see that at a glance. But I hope you are not going to stop at that. It is very well for a beginning, but soon you will have enough of caricaturing. Study, learn to see and to paint, draw, make landscapes. They are so beautiful, the sea and the sky, the animals, the people and the trees, just as nature has made them, with their character, their real way of being, in the light, in the air, just as they are.'

"But the exhortations of Boudin did not take. The man, after all, was pleasing to me. He was earnest, sincere, I felt it but I could not digest his painting, and when he offered to take me with him to sketch in the fields, I always found a pretext to politely decline. Summer came—my time was my own—I could make no valid excuse—weary of resisting, I gave in at last, and Boudin, with untiring kindness, undertook my education. My eyes, finally, were opened, and I really understood nature; I learned at the same time to love it. I analyzed it in its forms with a pencil, I studied it in its colorations. Six months later, in spite of the entreaties of my mother, who had begun to seriously worry because of the company I kept, and who thought me lost in the society of a man of such bad repute as Boudin, I announced to my father that I wished to become a painter and that I was going to settle down in Paris to learn.

"'You shall not have a cent!'

"'I will get along without it.'"

Setting Out for Paris

"Indeed I could get along without it. I had long since made my little pile. My caricatures had done it for me. I had often in one day executed seven or eight caricature-portraits. At twenty francs apiece, my receipts had been large, and I had made it a practice from the start to entrust my earnings to one of my aunts, keeping but paltry sums for pocket money. At sixteen one feels rich with two thousand francs. I obtained from several picture lovers who protected Boudin . . . some letters of introduction and set out post-haste for Paris.

"It took me some little time at first to decide on my line of action. I called on the artists to whom I had letters. I received from them excellent advice; I received also some very bad advice. Did not [painter consultant] Troyon want me to enter the studio of [painter Thomas] Couture? It is needless to tell you how decided was my refusal to do so. I admit even that it cooled me, temporarily at least, in my esteem and admiration for Troyon. I began to see less and less of him, and, after all, connected myself only with artists who were seeking. At this juncture, I met [Camille] Pissarro, who was not then thinking of posing as a revolutionist, and who was tranquilly working in [Jean-Baptiste-Camille] Corot's style. The model was excellent; I followed his example, but during my whole stay in Paris, which lasted four years, and during which time I frequently visited Hâvre, I was governed by the advice of Boudin, although inclined to see nature more broadly."

Off to the Army

"I reached my twentieth year. The hour for conscription was about to strike. I saw its approach without fear. And so did my family. They had not forgiven me my flight; they had let me live as I chose during those four years, only because they thought they would catch me when the time came for me to do military duty. They thought that once my wild oats were sown, I would tame down sufficiently to return home, readily enough, and bend at last to commerce. If I refused, they would stop my allowance, and if I drew an unlucky number they would let me go.

"They made a mistake. The seven years of service that appalled so many were full of attraction for me. A friend who was in the regiment of the *Chasseurs d'Afrique* and who adored military life, had communicated to me his enthusiasm and inspired me with his love of adventure. Nothing attracted me so much as the endless calvacades under the burning sun, the *razzias*, the crackling of gunpowder, the sabre thrusts, the nights in the desert under a tent, and I replied to my father's ultimatum with a superb gesture of indifference. I drew an unlucky number. I succeeded by personal insistence, in being drafted into an African regiment and started out.

"In Algeria, I spent two really charming years. I incessantly saw something new; in my moments of leisure I attempted to render what I saw. You cannot imagine to what extent I increased my knowledge, and how much my vision gained thereby. I did not quite realize it at first. The impressions of light and color that I received there were not to classify themselves until later; but they contained the germ of my future researches."

An Unexpected Break

"I fell ill at the end of two years, and quite seriously. They sent me home to recuperate. Six months of convalescence were spent in drawing and painting with redoubled energy. Seeing me thus persisting, worn as I was by the fever my father became convinced that no will could curb me, that no ordeal would get the better of so determined a vocation, and as much from lassitude as from fear of losing me, for the Doctor had led him to expect this, should I return to Africa, he decided, towards the end of my furlough to buy me out.

"'But it is well understood,' he said to me, 'that this time you are going to work in dead earnest. I wish to see you in an *atelier*, under the discipline of a well-known master. If you resume your independence, I will stop your allowance without more ado. Is it a bargain. This arrangement did not more then half suit me, but I felt that it was necessary not to oppose my father when he for once entered into my plans. I accepted. It was agreed that I should have at Paris and in the person of the painter Toulmouche, who had just married one of my cousins, an artistic tutor, who would guide me and furnish regular reports of my labors."

Painting What You See

"I landed one fine morning at Toulmouche's with a stock of studies which he declared pleased him very much. 'You have a future,' he said, 'but you must direct your efforts in some given channel. You will enter the studio of [Charles] Gleyre. He is the staid and wise master that you need.' And grumbling, I placed my easel in the studio full of pupils, over which presided this celebrated artist. The first week I worked there most conscientiously, and made with as much application as spirit a study of nude from the living model, that Gleyre corrected on Mondays. The following week, when he came to me, he sat down, and solidly planted on my chair, looked attentively at my production. Then—I can see him yet—he turned round, and leaning his grave head to one side with a satisfied air, said to me: 'Not bad! not bad at all, that thing there, but it is too much in the character of the model—you have before you a short thickset man, you paint him short and thickset—he has enormous feet, you render them as they are. All that is very ugly. I want you to remember, young man, that when one executes a figure, one should always think of the antique. Nature, my friend, is all right as an element of "study" but it offers no interest. Style, you see, style is everything.'

"I saw it all. Truth, life, nature, all that which moved me, all that which constituted in my eyes the very essence, the only *raison d' être* of art, did not exist for this man. I no longer wished to remain under him. I felt that I was not born to begin over again in his wake the *Illusions Perdues* and other kindred bores. Therefore, why persist?"

Congenial Companions

"I nevertheless waited several weeks. In order not to exasperate my family, I continued to appear regularly at the studio, remaining only just long enough to execute a rough sketch from the model, and to be present at inspection, then I skipped. Moreover, I had found in the studio congenial companions, natures far from commonplace. They were [Pierre-Auguste] Renoir and [Alfred] Sisley, whom I was never thereafter to lose sight of—and [Jean-Frédéric] Bazille, who immediately became my chum, and who would have become noted had he lived. None of them manifested, any more than I did, the least enthusiasm for a mode of teaching that antagonized both their logic and their temperament. I forthwith preached rebellion to them. The exodus being decided on, we left, Bazille and I taking a studio in common.

"I forgot to tell you, that a short time before, I had made the acquaintance of [painter Johan] Jongkind. During my furlough of convalescence, one fine afternoon I was working in the neighborhood of Hâvre, in a farm. A cow was grazing in the meadow; I conceived the idea of making a drawing of the good beast. But the good beast was capricious, and every moment was shifting its position. My easel in one hand, my stool in the other, I, following, was trying with more or less success to regain my point of view. My evolutions must have been very amusing, for I heard a hearty burst of laughter behind me. I turned round and beheld a puffing colossus. But the colossus was good natured. 'What a minute,' he said, 'I will help you.' And the colossus in huge strides, comes up with the cow, and grabbing her by the horns, tries to make her pose. The cow, unused to such treatment, takes it in bad part. It was now my turn to laugh. The colossus, quite discomfited, lets go the beast and comes over to chat with me.

"He was an Englishman, a visitor, very much in love with painting and very well posted on what was going on in our country:

"'So, you make landscapes,' he said.

"'Well, yes.'

"'Do you know Jongkind?'

"'No, but I have seen his work.'

"'What do you think of it?'

"'It is very strong.'

"'Right you are. Do you know he is here?'

"'You don't say!'

"'He lives in Honfleur. Would you like to know him?'

"'Decidedly yes. But then you are one of his friends?'

"'I have never see him, but as soon as I learned of his presence, I sent him my card. It is an opening wedge. I am going to invite him to lunch with you.'"

Lunch with Jongkind

"To my great surprise the Englishman kept his promise, and the following Sunday we were all three lunching together. Never was there a merrier feast. In the open air, in a country garden, under the trees, in presence of good rustic cooking, his glass well filled, seated between two admirers whose sincerity was above suspicion, Jongkind was beside himself with contentment. The impromptu of the adventure amused him; moreover he was not accustomed to being thus sought after. His painting was too new and in a far too artistic strain to be then, in 1862, appreciated at its true worth. Neither was there ever any one so modest and retiring. He was a simple good-hearted man, murdering French atrociously, and very timid. That day he was very talkative. He asked to see my sketches, invited me to come and work with him, explained to me the why and the wherefore of his manner and thereby completed the teachings that I had already received from Boudin. From that time on he was my real master, and it was to him that I owed the final education of my eye."

"I frequently saw him again in Paris. My painting, need I say it, gained by it. I made rapid progress. Three years later, I exhibited. The two marines that I had sent were received with highest approval and hung on the line in a fine position. It was a great success.—Same unanimity of praise in 1866, for a large portrait that you have seen at Durand-Ruel's for a long time, the "Woman in Green." The papers carried my name even to Hâvre. My family at last gave me back their esteem. With their esteem came also a resumption of my allowance. I floated in opulence, temporarily at least, for later on we were to quarrel again, and I threw myself body and soul into the *plein air.*

"It was a dangerous innovation. Up to that time no one had indulged in any, not even [painter Édouard] Manet, who only attempted it later, after me. His painting was still very classical and

I have never forgotten the contempt that he showed for my beginnings. It was in 1867; my manner had shaped itself, but, after all, it was not revolutionary in character. I was still far from having adopted the principle of the subdivision of colors that set so many against me, but I was beginning to try my hand at it partially and I was experimenting with effects of light and color that shocked accepted customs. The jury that had received me so well at first, turned against me and I was ignominiously blackballed when I presented this new painting to the Salon."

An Old Grudge

"Still I found a way to exhibit, but elsewhere. Touched by my entreaties, a dealer, who had his shop in the Rue Auber, consented to display in his window a Marine that had been refused at the *Palais de l'Industrie*. There was a general hue and cry. One evening, that I had stopped in the street, in the midst of a group of loungers, to listen to what was being said about me, I saw Manet coming along with two or three of his friends. They stopped to look, and Manet, shrugging his shoulders, cried disdainfully: 'Just look at this young man who attempts to do the *plein air!* As if the ancients had ever thought of such a thing!'

"Moreover, Manet had an old grudge against me. At the Salon of 1866, on varnishing day, he had been received from the very moment of his entrance, with such acclamations as: 'Excellent, my boy, your picture!' And then hand-shakings, bravos and felicitations. Manet, as you may well believe it, was exultant. What was not his surprise, when he noticed that the canvas, about which he was being congratulated was by me! It was the "Woman in Green." The saddest part of it all was that in hurriedly taking his leave he should fall upon a group of painters among which were Bazille and I. 'How goes it?' said one of the crowd. 'Ah! my boy, it is disgusting, I am furious. I am being complimented only on a painting that is not by me. One would think it is a mystification.'

"When Astruc told him the next day that he had given vent to his ill humour before the very author of the picture, and when he offered to introduce me to him, Manet, with a sweeping gesture, refused. He felt bitter towards me on account of the trick I had unconsciously played upon him. Only once had he been congratulated for a master-stroke and that master-stroke had been made by another. How bitter it must have been for a sensitiveness always bared to the quick as his was!"

The Meeting of Minds

"It was in 1869 only that I saw him again, but then we at once became fast friends. At our first meeting he invited me to join him every evening in a café of the *Batignolles*, where he and his friends gathered after working hours, to talk. There I met [Henri] Fantin-Latour and [Paul] Cézanne, [Edgar] Degas, who soon after arrived from Italy, the art critic [Edmond] Duranty, Emile Zola who was then making his *début* in literature, and several others. For my part I took there Sisley, Bazille and Renoir. Nothing could be more interesting then these *causeries* with their perpetual clash of opinions. They kept our wits sharpened, they encouraged us in sincere and disinterested research, they provided us with stores of enthusiasm that for weeks and weeks kept us up, until the final shaping of the idea was accomplished. From them we emerged tempered more highly, with a firmer will, with our thoughts clearer and more distinct.

"[The Franco-Prussian War] was declared with Germany. I had just married. I went over to England. . . . I suffered want. England did not care for our paintings. It was hard. By chance I ran across [Charles-François] Daubigny, who formerly had manifested some interest in me. He was then painting scenes on the Thames that pleased the English very much. He was moved by my distress. 'I see what you need,' he said; 'I am going to bring a dealer to you.' The next day I made the acquaintance of Mr. Durand-Ruel.

"And Mr. Durand-Ruel for us was a saviour. During fifteen years and more, my paintings and those of Renoir, Sisley and Pissarro had no other outlet but through him. The day came when he was compelled to restrict his orders, make his purchases less frequent. We thought ruin stared us in the face: but it was the advent of success. . . . Our works found buyers. . . . The public began to find them less bad. At Durand-Ruel's the collectors would have none of them. Seeing them in the hands of other dealers they grew more confident. They began to buy. The momentum was given. To-day nearly everyone appreciates us in some degree."

The Trail to the Little Bighorn

by Herman J. Viola

The Battle of the Little Bighorn, commonly know as "Custer's Last Stand," was an American military engagement fought on June 25, 1876, in the Montana Territory. On the morning of June 25, soldiers of the elite U.S. Seventh Cavalry led by Lieutenant George Armstrong Custer attacked a large Sioux and Northern Cheyenne Indian encampment on the banks of the Little Bighorn River. By day's end, Custer and more than two hundred of his men lay dead. The battle was part of a major army campaign to fully eradicate the Indians, or at least bring them into submission. After the Battle of the Little Bighorn, the fate of the Native Americans was sealed and changed forever. The battle marked the end of a way of life the Native Americans had known for centuries.

The army's campaign was centered in southeastern Montana Territory. Custer's regiment of 655 men formed the advance guard of a force under General Alfred Howe Terry (1827–1890). Custer was known as a rebellious and fierce soldier. Filled with arrogance and determination and often disregarding orders and acting on his own instincts, Custer was known to charge into battle with his troops even when the odds were sharply against him. This is precisely what happened at the Little Bighorn. Unlike earlier battles, Custer did not make it out of the Little Bighorn alive.

On June 25, Custer's scouts located the Sioux on the Little Bighorn River. Unaware of the overwhelming strength of the Indians and despite the repeated warnings of his scouts, Custer disregarded orders to join General Terry and attacked at once. After meeting the more than three thousand Indians at the river, Custer's troops were quickly surrounded and despite a desperate fight, all were killed. The battlefield was established as the Little Bighorn National Monument in 1886.

Herman J. Viola is a curator emeritus of the Smithsonian Institution and former director of the Smithsonian's National Anthropological Archives. The following essay is from his book *It Is a Good Day to Die*. In it, Indian eyewitnesses describe their experience in the Battle of the Little Bighorn. Viola is also the author of numerous articles, essays, and books on Native American culture, history, and anthropology.

I am an old man, and soon my spirit must leave this earth to join the spirits of my fathers. Therefore, I shall speak only the truth in telling what I know of the fight on the Little Horn River where General Custer was killed. Curly, who was with us, will tell you that I do not lie.

This is how White Man Runs Him, a member of the Crow Indian tribe, replied to questions about his part in the famous battle known to generations of white Americans as "Custer's Last Stand." He had been a young warrior, only about eighteen years old, when he agreed to help the U.S. Army find and fight the Lakota and Cheyennes, who were bitter enemies of his Crow people. With White Man Runs Him were five other Crow warriors serving as scouts for Custer's Seventh Cavalry. Curly was one of them. They survived the battle, but Custer and more than 250 troopers did not. Fought on June 25, 1876, the Battle of the Little Bighorn River—or the "Greasy Grass," as it was known to the Plains Indians—was a dramatic victory for the Lakota and Cheyenne peoples over the U.S. government.

In their old age, the former scouts and Lakota and Cheyenne veterans of the battle were often questioned by reporters, historians, and other individuals curious to know exactly what had taken place at the battle. How was it that the Indians, whom most whites believed to be undisciplined and poorly armed, were able to defeat one of the finest fighting forces in the U.S. Army? Was it poor leadership by Custer? Was it widespread panic and fear by inexperienced soldiers? Was it the clever generalship of Sitting Bull, who lured Custer into an elaborate trap? Or was it the Everywhere Spirit, fulfilling a prediction made to Sitting Bull, who had had a vision during the Sun Dance of soldiers falling upside down into his village?

Only the Indians Survived

The Northern Cheyennes still believe the victory was due to Custer's failure to keep a promise made almost a decade earlier to their kinsmen, the Southern Cheyennes of Oklahoma. In 1869, after fighting and defeating the Southern Cheyennes, Custer smoked a pipe of peace with Cheyenne leaders. As part of the ceremony, Custer made a promise never to make war on the Cheyennes again. The Cheyenne chiefs warned him that if he failed to listen carefully to their words and failed to keep this solemn vow, great harm would befall him. That is why, after his body was found and recognized on the battlefield, two Cheyenne women punctured his ears with their sewing awls. They did this to help him hear better in the afterlife—because he had obviously failed to hear, or heed, the warning their chiefs had made in 1869.

At first, Indian veterans of the battle refused to tell their stories out of fear of punishment by the U.S. government. Even today, some descendants of the Lakota and Cheyennes who fought that day are reluctant to tell outsiders the stories about the battle that they heard from their parents and grandparents. Even when Indians talked about the battle, army investigators and historians tended to discredit their accounts, believing that they were somehow trying to conceal the truth. Now, after the passage of so many years, this attitude has changed. The Indians' stories are acknowledged as providing a vivid picture of events that day. And because none of the soldiers with Custer lived to tell what happened, theirs is the only account that survives.

The followers of Sitting Bull, Gall, and Crazy Horse fought as individuals, not as members of military units like a troop of cavalry, and their stories are individual versions of events. Because the Indian village was caught by surprise, there was no overall battle plan. Each woman, child, and warrior had only a personal perspective of the battle. It requires the comparison of many individual stories to obtain some idea of what happened. In truth, there was a great deal of confusion. Clouds of dust thrown up by galloping horses and the black smoke from hundreds of gunshots obscured everything. At the height of the battle it was hard to tell Indian from white man. Therefore, no precise accounting of what happened during the battle will ever be possible.

Most of the individuals who appear in this [essay] told their stories many years after the battle. Even in their old age, however, they had vivid memories of that June day in 1876 when Custer and the Seventh Cavalry surprised the followers of Sitting Bull in their camp along the banks of the Greasy Grass.

A New Way of Life

The trail to the Greasy Grass began in the 1840s, when the first white settlers starred crossing the Great Plains in their covered wagons, seeking homes in the fertile valleys of California and Oregon. The small trickle of settlers eventually became a torrent, thanks to the construction of railroads and government initiatives such as the 1862 Homestead Act, which gave land free to homesteaders.

As the flow of settlers increased, Indians across the West tried to defend their land and their way of life. Among the Lakota people of the northern Great Plains, the Santee, who lived in present-day Minnesota, fought an unsuccessful campaign against settlers and the U.S. Army in 1862. Defeated by the superior firepower and numbers of the army, some of the Santee fled west to join Lakota bands living in the Dakota Territory.

More successful was Red Cloud, a leader of the Oglala, whose two-year fight against the U.S. Army forced the government to abandon forts built along the Bozeman Trail, which ran through Lakota hunting grounds in what is now eastern Montana and Wyoming. At Fort Laramie, Wyoming, in 1868, Red Cloud and other Lakota leaders signed a treaty that temporarily ended hostilities on the northern plains and created the Great Sioux Reservation, in what is now South Dakota, west of the Missouri River. The treaty also gave the Lakota permission to continue to use their traditional hunting grounds as long as the buffalo and other game animals were plentiful enough to feed them. However, the chiefs who signed the treaty—including Red Cloud—agreed to one day accept life on reservations, where they would receive food, clothes, money, cattle, and farm supplies from government officials called Indian agents. On the reservations, teachers, missionaries, and farmers would instruct the Indians in a new way of life.

Sitting Bull, leader of the Hunkpapa band of the Lakota, did not sign the Treaty of Fort Laramie. He and other leaders, such as Crazy Horse, instead chose the life of their fathers, moving their villages from place to place and hunting the buffalo. "I am a red man," Sitting Bull proclaimed. "If the Great Spirit had desired me to be a white man, he would have made me so in the first place. It is not necessary for eagles to be crows. Now we are poor, but we are free. I do not wish to be shut up in a corral. All reservation Indians I have seen are worthless. They are neither red warriors not white farmers. They are neither wolf nor dog."

The Deadline Passes

Soon after the Fort Laramie Treaty was signed, white settlers began to press closer to the Great Sioux Reservation. The once-unlimited buffalo herds, upon which the Plains Indians depended for their livelihood, became harder and harder to find. Surveyors began illegally mapping railroad routes across Indian land, including the Great Sioux Reservation. Then, in 1874, the government sent a scientific expedition into the Black Hills, an area to the west of the Great Sioux Reservation that was—and is to this day—sacred to the Lakota and Cheyenne Indians. The expedition, which was led by Lieutenant Colonel George Armstrong Custer, found gold in the Black Hills. Prospectors soon overran the region, and the army faced a losing struggle trying to keep them off Indian land. After an effort to buy the Black Hills failed, the government accused Sitting Bull, Crazy Horse, Gall, and the independent Lakota bands of having violated the Treaty of Fort Laramie. Late in 1875, the government sent messengers to all the free-roaming bands: "Come to the reservation or be considered hostiles against whom the United States Army will make war."

When the deadline of January 31, 1876, passed and the Indians did not come onto the reservations, the U.S. Army made good the threat. Between March and May 1876, it sent three columns of soldiers to Montana un-

George Armstrong Custer

der General George Crook, Colonel John Gibbon, and General Alfred Terry. Their orders were to find the Indians and force them onto the Great Sioux Reservation. In March 1876, after Crook attacked a Cheyenne camp on the Powder River, Lakota and Cheyenne bands began camping together for mutual protection from the soldiers. Their strength was further increased by warriors from the reservation—young men who heard that Sitting Bull wanted to drive the white men from the Black Hills and who were eager to earn honors in battle.

The Indians were not anxious to fight, but neither were they afraid of the soldiers. They were well armed. Indeed, many of them carried better rifles than those issued to the army. The Indians were also proud, defiant, and superbly led by the charismatic Sitting Bull and the brilliant war chief Crazy Horse. Other important chiefs were Gall and Hump of the Lakota and Dull Knife, Lame White Man, and Two Moon of the Cheyennes. Their confidence was bolstered by a vision Sitting Bull had while undergoing the Sun Dance, in which he saw many dead soldiers "falling right into our camp."

Too Many Warriors for Custer

On June 17, scouts brought word to Crazy Horse that soldiers were marching toward their camp along the nearby Rosebud Creek. Crazy Horse met them with a large force of Lakota and Cheyenne warriors. The Battle of the Rosebud lasted six hours and ended only after the Indians got tired of fighting. What saved Crook's infantry from disaster was the vigilance and bravery of his Indian allies—Shoshone and Crow scouts whose skilled horsemanship stopped a Lakota and Cheyenne surprise attack and kept them at bay while the soldiers got into battle formation.

Meanwhile, Gibbon and Terry, unaware of Crook's defeat, met on the Yellowstone River at the mouth of the Rosebud. Terry sent some six hundred cavalry under Lieutenant Colonel Custer to follow a fresh Indian trail leading to the Bighorn River. With Custer were six Crow and forty Arikara scouts. Custer's orders were to locate the village and wait for reinforcements. Meanwhile, the infantry with Gibbon and Terry would follow as quickly as possible and then attack the village from at least two directions so the Indians would be unable to escape.

The Crow and Arikara scouts easily found the village, but warned Custer that there were too many warriors in it and that his tired cavalry should not risk an attack. They urged him to wait for the expected reinforcements.

The village was indeed huge. It held some twelve hundred tepees in six large tribal circles. Five circles belonged to Lakota tribal bands—Hunkpapa, Oglala, Miniconjou, Sans Arc, Blackfeet—and one was Northern Cheyenne. The village stretched along the Greasy Grass for approximately three miles. In the village were upward of ten thousand people, including as many as two thousand fighting men. The horse herd was gigantic—twenty-five thousand head.

Custer feared that the Indians would slip away if he waited for Gibbon and Terry, so despite his scouts' warnings, he decided to attack at once. At noon on June 25, he divided his force into three units, leaving a few troopers to guard the mule train laden with supplies and extra ammunition. One unit, under Captain Frederick Benteen, was sent to cut off the escape of Indians to the left of the village. A second unit, under Major Marcus Reno, was ordered to attack the village directly. Custer's unit swung around to the right of the village, expecting to attack it from another direction while the Indians were occupied with Reno. The key to Custer's strategy appears to have been the expectation that most of the Indians in the village would run away rather than fight.

Reno charged the village as ordered, but the warriors did not run away. Instead, they rushed forward, in order to give their families time to get out of the village and seek refuge in the nearby hills. As a result, Reno's troopers quickly found themselves confronted by hundreds of angry warriors led by Chief Gall of the Hunkpapa. Gall was the adopted brother of Sitting Bull and an able war chief. During Reno's attack, Gall's two wives and three children were killed because their tent was close to the scene of the fighting.

The Indians stopped Reno's attack and then began to surround his outnumbered troopers, forcing them to make a hasty and disorderly dash to some bluffs along the river. Reno lost a third of his men during the retreat, although some managed to hide in bushes along the river and later rejoined their comrades under cover of darkness.

Crazy Horse's Bravery

Custer continued out of sight behind the bluffs along the river with the idea of attacking another portion of the village. When he finally got a good view of the camp, he sent an urgent message to Benteen: "Come on. Big village. Be quick. Bring [ammunition] packs." But Benteen never reached Custer. Instead, he joined Reno on the bluffs, where they spent the rest of the day pinned down by Indian rifle fire. The Indians kept up a relentless attack on the frightened soldiers until the next morning. Then, aware of the approach of reinforcements under Terry and Gibbon, the Lakota and the Cheyennes packed up their tents and moved away.

Custer tried to attack the village by crossing the Greasy Grass at Medicine Tail Coulee, which provided a path for horsemen midway into the village, but Indian sharpshooters forced the soldiers back. Custer and his officers then had the troops form a large, uneven defensive square while they waited for the reinforcements that never came. Meanwhile, seeing that Benteen and Reno were content to remain on the bluffs, most of the warriors at that front rushed back to confront Custer.

A warrior who played a key role in the destruction of Custer's command was Crazy Horse, one of the most respected and revered of the Lakota leaders. In battle his hair flowed freely, with a single eagle feather hanging tip down. His face paint was a red zigzag line with white spots that symbolized the lightning and hail of the thunder spirits. Crazy Horse's medicine—his spiritual power—was so strong that it was believed no bullet could touch him. At a critical moment in the battle, mounted on his buckskin pinto and blowing an eagle-bone whistle, he dashed back and forth across a line of Custer's dismounted troops, daring them to shoot him. Each time he rode past, the soldiers fired and missed with their single-shot carbines. "I will pass before them a third time," Crazy Horse yelled to his followers, who were shielded by thick sagebrush. "As soon as they shoot their guns, rush forward before they have time to reload."

Inspired by Crazy Horse's bravery, the hidden Indians dashed forward. Many of Custer's soldiers panicked and began to run toward the center of the defensive square. The troopers melted away as the Lakota and Cheyennes rushed among them, hitting them with clubs and tomahawks. One of the Lakota veterans later remarked, "It was like hunting buffalo."

The Story of Louis Dog

by Florence Whiteman, as told to Herman J. Viola

Florence Whiteman lives near the town of Lame Deer on the Northern Cheyenne Reservation. At the age of twelve Whiteman was inducted into the Cheyenne Elk Warriors Society, a special honor normally reserved for young men believed to have special abilities as warriors, and she is the last living woman warrior among the Northern Cheyenne. Raised by her grandparents, she is also the last Cheyenne woman married in the traditional Cheyenne way in 1943, when she was fifteen years old. Because of her special status as an elk warrior, her marriage was arranged for her. Louis Dog, Whiteman's grandfather, knew many men who had fought U.S. Army general George Armstrong Custer. He also knew many stories and had firsthand experience with Custer attacking his own village.

Like many other Cheyenne, Sioux, and Lakota warriors, Louis Dog became a scout for the U.S. Army at Fort Keogh, Montana. He knew many stories about Custer and the Indian warriors. There were many skirmishes between the whites and the Indians, but none so bloody and deadly as the Battle of the Little Bighorn. Custer was known to the Indians as a fierce and fearless warrior. Many Indians both feared and respected him for his courage on the battlefield. In the following selection, Florence Whiteman relays some stories told to her by her grandfather, Louis Dog, about Custer and how the Indian warriors prepared themselves for battle.

Herman J. Viola is curator emeritus of the Smithsonian Institution and the former director of the Smithsonian's National Anthropological Archives. Viola is the author of more than fifteen books,

including *Little Bighorn Remembered: The Untold Indian Story of
Custer's Last Stand.* The following story from the book was relayed
to Viola by Whiteman.

My name is Florence Whiteman. My first husband was
named Waters. When I was about three years old, my
mother took me to my grandmother and gave me to her
to raise. That's the Cheyenne tradition. The firstborn is raised by
the grandparents. I thought when I was five years old that my
mother didn't love me, that my mother threw me away to my
grandmother. But she had a reason to do what she did.

My grandfather Louis Dog was one hundred years old when
he died. His Cheyenne name was Ho-ta Me-he, "dog" in
Cheyenne. After the [General George Armstrong] Custer battle
[Little Bighorn], he joined the Army as a scout at Fort Keogh.
Later on, the government built him a house on his land near
Busby because he was a veteran. When he died, the people came
to get him in a hearse. They brought him a coffin. They brought
him an American flag and they embalmed him. They took care
of him. They gave him the flag and they put him in uniform, and
then they put him in the coffin. I thought that was something
good, you know, that they were doing this for him, these white
people. I thought he must have earned it some way.

A Lesson for Custer

I grew up with my grandfather, and he taught me things about
Cheyenne culture. He wouldn't even go anywhere. He was an
old man. I didn't realize at the time how old he was. Early in the
morning he would get me up and I would go with him. We would
go get his horses. He had two horses. As soon as they saw him
the horses would come running to him because they knew he was
out there to greet them. And he would stand there and talk to
them, in Cheyenne.

I learned Cheyenne pretty well from both my grandparents.
But my grandmother had lost her hearing by then. She said it was
because she had performed some ceremony and did not live up
to the rules. She said the medicine man warned her that would
happen if she didn't follow the rules. She slowly lost her hearing. She couldn't hear, so I had to communicate with her in sign
language. I got to know pretty good sign language from her and

from my grandfather. That was the only way we could communicate with each other.

My grandfather told me that Custer had met the Cheyennes before. He had talked with them in Oklahoma. They had a meeting with Custer to make peace. At the meeting they smoked the pipe. All of them, the chiefs and Custer, they smoked the pipe. The chiefs told him that they were going to become friends, because they were smoking a pipe. They explained this to Custer. After Custer got all through smoking this pipe, there was nothing left in it but ashes. The chiefs then told him to stand up. He had his boots on. They told him to take that pipe and tap it on his boots, so the ashes could come out of the pipe and fall on the ground. Then they told him to take the sole of his boot and rub the ashes into the ground, so that's what he did. The chiefs then said, "Now, if you ever double-cross the Cheyenne, that's how you're going to end up. That's the purpose of smoking the pipe and rubbing those ashes into the ground. There's going to be nothing left of you, if you ever double-cross the Cheyenne." And that's what happened to him at Little Bighorn. That happened because he probably didn't believe us. That's the way it was back then. Whatever the medicine men said at the time after they did ceremonies, it always, always came true. That's one of the stories my grandfather told me.

The Bravest Warrior

My grandfather thought Custer was the greatest—the way he looked, the way he acted. He thought Custer could have been one of the best warriors. I guess he was.

My grandfather said he could always tell who was going to become the best warrior. He told me about a little boy the Cheyennes captured once when they attacked a Ute camp. There was this little boy standing around crying. You know how it is. One of the Cheyennes picked up the little boy and took him home on his horse. When the chiefs saw what happened, they said to the warrior, "Go give this little boy to an old lady to raise, a grandmother. We'll raise him as a Cheyenne. We won't tell him that he's from another tribe. We'll raise him as a Cheyenne and see what happens." Well, this little boy was raised by the grandmother. He was raised like a Cheyenne. Everybody watched him grow up because they knew he was not a Cheyenne. But he turned out to be the best of them.

My grandfather said on the day Custer came to attack their village, the Cheyennes had runners watching in the hills. This boy was one of the runners. He came running down to warn the village that soldiers were coming. He told them how far away Custer was and what part of the day he was going to be there. He could tell by the sun. When the sun gets to here, that's when the soldiers are going to come riding.

These runners—there were two of them—used this root that grows out here. It glows blue at night. They use that. They put it on their ears, on their arms. It makes them strong. It's Indian medicine. They used it when they had ceremonies like the Contrary Ceremony. They would use it, too, to represent animals. The medicine men put that root on these two runners. When they put their ears to the ground, the runners could hear those hooves coming. They could analyze how far away Custer was. And they could see from that point those flashing buttons on their coats. One of the boys ran down to the village and one stayed up there. The runner told them, "This is how far away they are."

Some of the warriors were down by the river in sweat lodges. They were sweating. Someone sent the Crazy Dogs to go down and tell them to get out of there and to get ready. The Crazy Dogs also took the Sacred Hat Keeper, some of the girls and boys, and some families up into the hills where they would be safe, where they wouldn't be hurt in case the warriors all got killed. The Cheyennes knew that's what Custer was determined to do, to kill all the Cheyennes. So they left. The old people and the children, they went out of the village, but the warriors came running.

Preparing for Battle

As the warriors were running around getting ready, a man got up and took his drum and began singing. He was singing the Suicide Song. And all these warriors who were getting ready, they were putting on their best moccasins, so that they could die in their best. They were getting their horses ready too. They came running to this man who was playing the Suicide Song. They began dancing to the song. If you dance to that Suicide Song, it means you must stay out there to the very end, because you have made a vow to win or die. That's the purpose of the Suicide Song.

Today if anyone sings that Suicide Song, we would probably all head for the hills because we're different now, you know! But at that time, those young men came running over and began

dancing. Some young girls, when they saw their brother dancing, why they said, "I'm going to go join my brother. I'll die with
my brother today." Some of the first ones did that, not that many.
Most of the young women took care of the old ladies, the elder-
lies, and the children. That was their job.

My grandfather said that Ute boy was the first one over there
dancing to the Suicide Song. Then he got on his horse and he
was leading the charge to meet Custer. This shows that he was
raised to be one of the best warriors that they could ever have as
a Cheyenne, but he wasn't a Cheyenne at all, he was a Ute. He
was the first one out there ready to meet the soldiers. He made
everyone proud. He showed everyone that old lady did a good
job raising him.

The Saddest Day

My grandfather said that when the fighting stopped some women
ran up there to see who was still alive, to see who died, to see
who needed help. Some of the dead were facing down, and they
were turning them over. I read in a book somewhere that Indian
women went through the pockets of the dead soldiers, robbing
these men. My grandfather never said anything like that. He said
they were worried, because someone might still be alive that
needed help, that might be just wounded. That's what they were
doing when they were out there. And he also said, "I really felt
bad that all those young people died, including white kids. From
what I seen of them, they were just young boys, like kids. They
had to die because of Custer." My grandfather felt sorry for them,
because they were forced to do what they did. He said that day
shouldn't have happened at all, that many people should not have
died. He said, "It still hurts me inside when I think about it." He
said he couldn't sleep for a long, long time after that. What happened that day was saddest thing that could ever happen.

The Final Rebellion at Kumamoto Castle

by James H. Buck

For many thousands of years, Japan existed in almost complete isolation from the outside world. The nation's customs, laws, and political system remained the same as they had been since well before the Middle Ages. A feudal system ruled by the shogun, society was a rigidly controlled pyramid with the peasants firmly at the bottom. The samurai, or military class, were the enforcers of the system, and it enjoyed a great deal of autonomy. After sustaining significant military threats from the West in 1854, Japan began a difficult period of modernization that would last more than twenty years.

Finally, in 1868, the shogunate was abolished and a new emperor, Mutsuhito, stepped into power under the title of Meiji ("Enlightened Peace"). Tokyo became the new capital, the army was modernized, industry grew, and Japan opened its doors to outside trade. Eventually, the old ways were left behind and it even became illegal to wear traditional dress and carry traditional weapons such as swords. This angered many Japanese, and over the following years these factionalists resisted modernization. One of the most significant revolts came from Satsuma province, an area of Japan that had a great deal of power during the shogunate and a very high population of samurai. The powerful Satsuma clan had been instrumental in establishing the Meiji emperor back in 1868, but now it was convinced that the process of modernization had gone too far.

The first significant test of the young Meiji government came in

1877. After nine years of working close to the central government, the samurai of Satsuma had grown dissatisfied with the direction the government was taking. Led by Saigo Takamori, they organized a considerable army to fight the untried troops of the central government. It was a momentous clash between traditional Japanese warfare as waged by the sword-wielding individual warriors and the new peasant army, trained in Western strategy and using Western weapons. The fighting was brief but bloody. Saigo and the Satsuma samurai fought well, but the government soldiers ultimately triumphed. Badly wounded, Saigo committed suicide in the traditional samurai tradition rather than be captured.

Saigo became a hero for the Japanese people. The emperor pardoned Saigo posthumously. Although samurai do not have any official status in Japan today, descendants of samurai families still enjoy high esteem among the Japanese population.

James H. Buck is a Japanese military historian and also the editor of *The Modern Japanese Military System*. In his introduction to the book *The True Story of the Siege of Kumamoto Castle*, excerpted here, he describes the events leading to the final rebellion of the samurai resistance against a modernized Meiji army and the major impact the Meiji had on Japanese society. The last holdout from a pre-Westernized Japan, the Satsuma samurai ultimately lost their battle, and those who survived saw Japan move permanently into the modern world.

The engagement [at Kumamoto Castle] was the turning point of the Civil War (Satsuma Rebellion) in Japan in 1877. The victory the Imperial Japanese Army scored in defeating the 54-day rebel siege of Kumamoto Castle made clear that military insurrection could not reverse the policies of the young oligarchy which took control of the government of Japan in the Meiji Restoration of 1868. Final defeat of the rebels was to take another five months after the siege was broken, but the issue was never in doubt thereafter. . . .

The martial qualities and military capacity of the despised "peasant soldiers" was an open question before this series of battles, but the conscripts proved themselves the equal of the *samurai* and traditional attitudes about the military profession in Japan were altered forever.

Some of those young officers who took part in the siege on the side of the Imperial Army rose to national and international prominence in later life in both civilian and military careers. . . . All of the major participants on the Satsuma side were killed in action. . . .

Kumamoto Castle was constructed during the years 1601 to 1607 by Kato Kiyomasa, lord of Higo (now Kumamoto Prefecture). In its present state of restoration, the castle has a circumference of nine kilometers and includes within its unique concave walls, two donjons, forty-nine turrets, and twenty-nine castle gates. . . .

At the time of the Satsuma Rebellion in 1877, Kumamoto was the second largest city on the island of Kyushu (next in size to Kagoshima)—a castle-town *(jokamachi)* of about 40,000 inhabitants. Today it is a metropolis of about 400,000 people and is the capital of Kumamoto Prefecture. It is located near Ariake Bay, about midway between the city of Kita-Kyushu (over 1,000,000 population) and Kagoshima (about 400,000), feudal capital of the Satsuma forces who sought passage through the Kumamoto Garrison in 1877. Refusal of the right of passage by the Imperial Army commander of Kumamoto was the event which precipitated the siege. . . .

A Decade of Change

The first decade of the Meiji Period (1868–1912) was crowded with epoch-making changes in nearly every aspect of Japanese life.

A group of young *samurai* from clans in western Japan seized control of the government of Japan from the House of Tokugawa which had ruled Japan with a feudal military dictatorship for two and one-half centuries. These young men consciously imposed from above a series of fundamental organizational and attitudinal changes on Japanese society designed to elevate Japan to the status of equality with the leading nations of the world—and to avoid a fate similar to that being suffered contemporaneously by China.

Little more than a century ago, Japan embarked on the purposeful transition from a loosely organized, feudal, agrarian country to a relatively centralized state in the initial stages of industrialization.

This process was necessary if Japan were to attain the power and status essential to continuity as a national entity. The new leadership came from the *samurai* class, the military-administrative elite of the *ancien régime;* paradoxically, this group was forced to make many sacrifices not commensurate with benefits received. In fact, the *samurai* leadership purposefully engaged in the unprecedented act of destroying its own class as a social entity in order to achieve its objective of unifying and then strengthening Japan for international leadership.

Transformation and Dissension

Among the far-reaching and even revolutionary changes undertaken by the Restoration government were these: reorganization of the central government and movement of the Imperial capital from Kyoto (where it had been for 1,100 years) to Edo (Tokyo); the abolition of the feudal clan organization and establishment of the prefecture system; revision of taxation; development of standard weights, measures, and coinage; and, most importantly for those *samurai* who resisted the new government led by their fellow *samurai*—the abolition of the traditional class system. The denial of the traditional social supremacy of the *samurai* class visibly meant the removal of the topknot and prohibition of the right to wear swords. The formal *déclassement* of the *samurai* was not acceptable to many, particularly those in the historically semi-autonomous clans of western Japan. The many actions of the new government were seen as cheaply selling the unique and valuable attributes of Japanese society. Such impressions were heightened by the nondiscriminatory and mass import of the material and intellectual paraphernalia of Western society.

Particularly galling to the declassed *samurai* was the early establishment of a military conscription system. It depended for manpower on the untutored farmer who was assigned duties and functions relative to the throne which had been for centuries the prerogative of *samurai*. *Samurai*, who previously had lived on stipends granted by feudal lords, were shifted to pensions payable by the central government. Forced commutation of these pensions in 1876 led to considerable financial loss for some *samurai*—and exacerbated the deeply felt psychic loss of social status and role as military careerist.

Among the strong clans of western Japan there was intra-clan dissension of serious magnitude, and this was reflected at central government levels. It focussed mainly in the more conservative ex-*samurai* elements who disapproved of policies adopted by the more progressive members of the government. Dissatisfaction stemmed not only from internal policies which harmed the *samurai* and altered traditional feudal relationships, but also from foreign policy differences. The specific case directly related to the Satsuma Rebellion was the controversy surrounding a proposal by conservative elements for a punitive expedition against Korea. The central figure in the advocacy of this course of action was Saigo Takamori, the leading figure from Satsuma in the Restoration, general in the army, state councillor, and commander of the Imperial Guards.

The Korean "Problem"

Soon after the Restoration of 1868, Japan sent a mission to Korea to announce that event. The Korean regent disapproved of Japan's own moves for internal renovation and refused to receive the Japanese emissary. Three missions were sent, but all failed to open relations with Korea even when the final mission was accompanied by two warships (late 1872). In May, 1873, Japan's foreign minister Soyejima led a mission to Peking (meeting with Saigo en route) and was granted an audience with the Manchu emperor. Soyejima concluded from his audience that China would not interfere in Korean affairs at that particular time. Returning to Japan in late July, 1872, Soyejima proposed the conquest of Korea as appropriate punitive action. But such a major decision could not be carried out until the return in September of the Iwakura Mission—a group of more than 100 Japanese who traveled in Europe and America from December, 1871, until September, 1873, to urge renegotiation of the unequal treaties Japan had signed with various Western countries.

The chief advocate of "war with Korea" was Saigo Takamori. He was supported by Soyejima, by several civilian politicians from the western clans, and by his fellow-clansmen—the Satsuma generals Kirino Toshiaki and Shinowara Kunimoto. This group formed a highly dangerous coterie essentially subversive to the plans for Japanese development advocated by the moderate progressives. Saigo's group combined narrow political self-interest with excessive "patriotism"—a combustible mixture.

This dissension about Korea was a reflection, and simultaneously the focus, of a major variance in beliefs of what best suited Japan's national interest. Saigo's group was conservative, even reactionary, and consisted of political opportunists who believed the national interest could best be served by aggression against

Korea. On the other hand, the group led by Iwakura believed Japan had to seek equality with the West by internal reform, modernization, and industrialization.

In any event, the group favoring concentration on internal stability and development carried the day. Saigo left the government, followed by his generals Kirino and Shinowara. Morale within the armed forces was struck a grievous blow. *Samurai* left government service and streamed to the west. The tenuous balance between the archconservative military and the progressive civilian parties had been upset. The seeds of a great civil war had been broadcast.

Those who had left government lacked cohesion, and clan loyalties were paramount for most. Political action as a means to alter government policy for them had failed. The recourse was to be a military rebellion of a limited and local nature.

Military Revolt—the Saga Uprising

Eto Shimpei, one of Saigo's supporters in the drive to punish Korea, quit the government and returned to his home province of Saga, about fifty miles north and slightly west of Kumamoto. He took leadership of about 2,500 ex-*samurai* who denounced the government using such slogans as "Punish Korea," "Restore the Feudal Lords to Their Proper Place," and "Expel Foreigners." Eto sought assistance from other dissident elements in Kyushu, but found none. Nevertheless, in February, 1874, his men made a daring move to seize Saga Castle by force. Temporarily successful, Eto's men were ignominiously defeated by fellow-clansmen serving in the Imperial Army garrison there. Within two months, the leaders were all rounded up and fifty of the participants were beheaded.

The Saga Rebellion is generally considered a minor affair by Western historians, but the revolt was not so considered by the Japanese government. The Imperial Army forces at that time numbered only 15,000, but more than 4,500 were actually used in the battle area to suppress the revolt, and an additional 4,000 were placed on full alert. More than half of the available Imperial Army forces were fully mobilized to deal with the insurrection. Casualties amounted to one-third of those suffered throughout the Sino-Japanese War of 1894–1895.

In an effort to ameliorate the discontent of some *samurai*, in April, 1874, the government undertook a punitive expedition against the aborigines of Formosa. This force of nearly 4,000 men was composed mainly of Satsuma warriors. The expedition was successful in that China was forced to recognize Japan's claim to the Ryukyu Islands and some *samurai* were more or less usefully employed and their discontent diverted temporarily. But, to men such as Saigo, the expedition was a poor substitute for a punitive expedition against Korea.

Three additional military revolts occurred in Kyushu in October, 1876. None had the support of Saigo. . . .

Developments in Kagoshima

After his withdrawal from the government in October, 1873, Saigo Takamori had remained aloof from both national political activity and local military revolt against the central government. He had returned to his home prefecture of Kagoshima, accompanied by about 600 of his soldiers and two of his major generals, Kirino and Shinowara. Many of those who went back to Kagoshima secured employment as local administrative officials. A number of them became instructors in the Private Schools, the most significant of Saigo's activities after his "retirement" in 1873.

The Main Private School *(Honko)* was founded in June, 1874, with financial support from awards made to Saigo and other Satsuma leaders for their services to the government during the Restoration War. Foreign instructors were hired to teach the English and French languages, but the core of the curriculum was the study of the Chinese classics and "spiritual training." Separate curricula were set up for the study of infantry and artillery tactics. All students took part in military exercises. By 1876, there were twelve "schools" in Kagoshima, and about 120 were established throughout the Satsuma territory. The total enrollment was about 7,000 students.

Saigo gave no instruction in the "schools." His personal influence on the students was through the guiding spirit of "spiritual" training. The basic principles of this training emphasized reverence for the emperor, compassion for the emperor's subjects, and readiness to offer one's life for the emperor.

Although Saigo remained detached from the conspiratorial activity of malcontent *samurai* in western Japan, some of the more impetuous of his followers had constantly urged military action against the government. Such agitation was a constant worry to the leaders of the "schools," for it was not certain that even Saigo's commanding personality could restrain them indefinitely.

For the first decade following the Restoration, Satsuma had resisted government control and isolated itself from developments in the rest of Japan. Strict precautions were taken by Satsuma leaders to deny the central government information on developments in Kagoshima Prefecture. Mutual isolation probably contributed to misunderstandings on both sides. The government overestimated the threat posed by the Private Schools; Satsuma overestimated the danger which the government posed to their survival.

Although the central government had quelled the uprisings in October, 1876, with relative ease, there was a gnawing concern with the potential danger posed by Saigo's "schools" and a continuing desire to bring the still semiautonomous Satsuma area into line with the other prefectures of Japan. This required internal administrative reform, and even before the revolts of October, 1876, the Satsuma area prefectural governor, Oyama Tsunayoshi, was called to Tokyo. He was told that reform had to take place within Kagoshima Prefecture and that men from other areas had to be introduced to effect the needed reforms. Governor Oyama eventually refused the government suggestion and offered to resign, but the central government insisted that he stay in office. Tokyo simultaneously threatened to carry out the reforms anyway.

Inspectors were sent into Kagoshima in late 1876, and reports rendered to the central government noted constant travelling by some of the Satsuma leaders and rumors of plots to take action against the Tokyo regime. Opinion was critical of the Tokyo authorities and hostility toward all outsiders was remarkable. And in Tokyo, there were newspaper articles detailing the government's concern about activity in Satsuma. Several years had passed since major reforms had been decreed by the Tokyo government, but still, it was said, Satsuma continued its old ways—refusing admission to outsiders, continuing to use the lunar calendar, and maintaining a private army in the form of the private schools. Satsuma was the only area in Japan which did not accept the direction of the central government.

The Immediate Causes of the Civil War of 1877

For generations prior to the Restoration of 1868, the Satsuma Clan had enjoyed relative freedom from outside intervention by the ruling military House of Tokugawa. In the years immediately preceding the opening of Japan, that clan had devoted about forty percent of its resources to the acquisition of military power. It had established a shipyard in Kagoshima, two weapons manufacturing plants, and three ammunuition depots. In 1871, these installations came under central government control, but their presence in Satsuma constituted military potential for use against the government. The government determined to reduce this potential by removing the arms and ammunition to a main government arsenal in Osaka. In January, 1877, the government attempted just this. No warning was given to the Kagoshima Prefecture government. The operation was begun in secret on January 30, 1877. An Imperial Navy crew, using a privately owned Mitsubishi ship, the *Sekiryu*, sought in a night attack to remove the munitions from the arsenal at Somuta. The operation was soon discovered and over 1,000 Satsuma men attacked and drove off the government force which fled empty-handed to Kobe. All government installations were then haughtily occupied by Satsuma men, and munitions seized from the government were openly paraded in Kagoshima. The counteroperation against the government was carried out entirely without the knowledge of Saigo.

Saigo was absent from Kagoshima when the munitions seizure was attempted, but returned to Kagoshima immediately upon notification. His return coincided with the detention of one Nakahara Misao, charged with plotting to assassinate Saigo.

An Assassination Plot Is Uncovered

Nakahara signed a "confession." This document seemed to reveal a plot which involved these elements. In December, 1876, Nakahara and others had talked with the chief inspector of the Tokyo Metropolitan Police (Kawaji Mitsukane, a native of Satsuma). The police chief noted the possibility of revolt in Kagoshima and said that if a revolt occurred, there was no recourse except to assassinate Saigo. Nakahara and others were to return to Kagoshima, try to subvert the local regime, and be ready to kill Saigo when the time arrived. The assassination would be followed by an attack by the central government military forces on the Satsuma capital.

The accuracy of the case made for the existence of the Tokyo-directed plot to assassinate Saigo will probably never be known.

Yet some aspects are beyond doubt. At least fifty members of the Tokyo Police Department who were natives of Satsuma did return to Kagoshima in late December, 1876, and early January, 1877; and their return did coincide with an inspection by a high Tokyo official. Their activities were closely screened and leaders in the Private Schools evaluated these activities as likely to lead to additional government action against Satsuma. Some advocated immediate execution of these "traitors" from the Tokyo Police Department. Local feeling against the actual and supposed acts of the central government intensified and was highlighted by fears of imminent government military action. *Samurai* from the outlying "schools" began to concentrate in Kagoshima and prepare for battle with government forces—without Saigo's encouragement—but hoping that eventually their heretofore passive leader would be forced to take command of them and lead them against the government.

The two events directly preceding and precipitating the Satsuma Rebellion of 1877 were the government's attempt to seize munitions in Kagoshima and the alleged plot against Saigo's life. Circumstances surrounding the attempted removal of munitions and the motives of the government in directing this action seem clear. But the matter of Nakahara's confession remains in doubt. Those implicated in the "plot" thereafter stoutly defended their innocence, and those who advocated rebellion were equally convinced of its authenticity.

Saigo decided to lead troops against the government. Certainly, the alleged "plot" was primary in his mind. The incidents related to the munitions seizure were apparently settled to Satsuma's satisfaction because the government personnel were driven away and Satsuma took direct control of the government military installations. For his part, Saigo criticized his subordinates for their counteraction against the government—at least he did so until he learned of the "assassination plot." Whether this knowledge in itself forced Saigo to act is not certain, but his decision did coincide with receipt of the information contained in Nakahara's "confession." When Saigo did act, it was with reluctance.

Movement to Contact

Three courses of action were considered by Saigo in his planning for means by which to clarify his relationship with the Tokyo authorities. The major possibilities were: (1) a personal visit by Saigo (accompanied by his generals Kirino and Shinowara and a body of Satsuma soldiers to Tokyo to talk with central government leaders); (2) the escort of Nakahara to Tokyo by some of Saigo's men for the same purpose; and (3) the dispatch of some of Saigo's subordinates with about 600 troops to Kyoto to attempt to talk with members of the emperor's party then sojourning there.

The first course of action was adopted. Saigo, or his subordinates, had dispatched to the Kumamoto Garrison commander a message requesting the right to pass through Kumamoto and calling upon the garrison commander to receive Saigo's command at the time of passage. This request was refused, but the Satsuma army was already on the march.

The main body of the Satsuma army marched north from Kagoshima on February 17, 1877, in a snowfall of seven inches, the most severe snowstorm seen in subtropical Kagoshima in half a century. Covering the 120 miles to Kumamoto in four days, the main body closed in near Kawashiri on February 21. The Satsuma army now mustered about 13,000 men just outside Kumamoto.

Within Kumamoto Castle, in late January, 1877, the Imperial Garrison consisted of about 2,000 troops of the Thirteenth Infantry Regiment.

In early February, the government took action to prepare for the possible rebellion by Saigo and was able to reinforce the garrison by 1,400 troops from the Fourteenth Infantry Regiment at Kokura and about 600 police. These elements closed in the castle on February 20. . . . The defending forces consisted of about 4,400 men (including support elements) and the besieging force of about 13,000.

The Castle Siege

The Satsuma plan of action was to employ about two-thirds of their strength in attacks on Kumamoto Castle from the southeast and from the northwest. About one-third was to be kept as a reserve, with some troops performing reconnaissance and security missions. Initial attempts to carry the castle were unsuccessful and eventually the castle was surrounded by the Satsuma troops. Reinforcing units of the Imperial Army soon arrived to break the siege and the major fighting by the Satsuma forces was to be against these Imperial troops pressing toward Kumamoto from the northwest, not mainly in attempts to take the castle. The continuous fighting in the Tabaruzaka sector during the first two weeks of March, 1877, was of unprecedented ferocity. The Imperial forces expended daily about 1,000 rounds of artillery and 320,000 rounds of small arms ammunition. Although the Imperial forces pushed the rebels part way back toward Kumamoto, the outcome was indecisive. In late March, a pincer movement was undertaken by an amphibious landing supported by naval gunfire from Ariake Bay, the landing being made at Yatsushiro, to the southwest of Kumamoto. A beachhead was secured. When reinforced further by Imperial troops, a coordinated attack was carried out against the rebel besiegers from the north and the south. This attack was successful in relieving the siege on April 14, 1877. During the 54-day siege, the garrison troops had suffered about twenty percent casualties.

The Course of the Rebellion After the Siege of Kumamoto Castle

The battle attendant on breaking the siege of the castle had cost both sides significant casualties. The story of the Civil War from mid-April until late September, 1877, is essentially that of successive dispersals and concentrations of Saigo's forces in other areas of southern Kyushu Island, marked by continually diminishing resources of the rebels and ever-increasing resources for the Imperial troops. Saigo masterfully evaded encirclement and destruction at Hitoyoshi, Miyakonojo, and Nobeoka, only to be cornered and defeated on his home ground of Kagoshima City.

When Saigo occupied the hill named Shiroyama in Kagoshima on September 2, 1877, his forces had dwindled to about 280 combatants and 80 coolies. Only fifty rifles remained. His troops had only two mortars, for which there was no ammunition.

Seven Imperial Army brigades and the Kumamoto Garrison were arrayed against this numerically insignificant force. The encirclement of Saigo's forces was completed on September 12. A general attack order was issued on the nineteenth. Thousands of rounds of artillery ammunition were expended to soften Saigo's positions and attempts were made to induce his surrender, but it was to no avail. The general attack was finally carried out at first light on September 24. By 6 A.M., only Saigo and forty of his men survived. Saigo had been wounded severely. Physically unable to enter combat, he decided to commit ritual suicide. Picking a spot, Saigo knelt toward the Imperial Palace and his sub-

ordinate Beppu Shinsuke sliced off his head. The remaining supporters plunged into the enemy line to their deaths. The Civil War
was ended by 7 A.M.

Some Observations

The Satsuma Rebellion pitted a well-trained *samurai* army imbued deeply with the traditional concepts of feudal Japan against
an army of "conscripted farmers" with relatively little training.
Militarily, the siege of Kumamoto Castle provided proof that the
despised conscript could protect Japan from its internal enemies.

The Imperial Army had several advantages—the ability to mobilize the resources of most of the nation, a continuing supply of
manpower, and overwhelming material superiority, especially in
weapons. It was innovative tactically, employing the railroad and
telegraph, using guerrilla and counterinsurgency units, and carrying out joint army-navy amphibious operations.

Perhaps the only advantages enjoyed by the Satsuma forces
were higher morale and better training. Generally unable to recruit men other than those who rebelled initially, Satsuma had to
carry on the war with an ever-diminishing number of men. Their
weapons were poor and no amount of *élan* or intrepidity can
compensate for the lack of arms.

Nevertheless, the Imperial Army required seven months to put
down the rebellion. Forced to mobilize about 60,000 soldiers, the
Imperial Army suffered about 16,000 casualties, some 7,000 of
whom died in combat or from wounds.

Militarily, it was a high price, but politically worth the cost. The
relief of the siege of Kumamoto Castle made it certain that the
young government established with the Restoration of 1868 could
maintain internal security. Victory in the Satsuma Rebellion elim-
inated the danger of armed internal revolt. The new government
had gained the freedom to continue its policies to develop a modern nation with an effective centralized administration.

The True Story of the Siege of Kumamoto Castle

by Takehiko Ideishi

At the time of the Satsuma Rebellion in 1877, Kumamoto was the second-largest city on the island of Kyushu and was protected by the grand and imposing Kumamoto Castle. Kumamoto Castle was built in 1607 and is among the three finest examples of feudal castle architecture in Japan. Still standing in a state of restoration, the castle has a circumference of nine kilometers, with forty-nine turrets and twenty-nine castle gates.

At the start of the rebel insurrection Saigo Takamori, leader of the Satsuma forces, sent advance notice to the Kumamoto garrison commander requesting the right to pass through Kumamoto and asked the garrison commander to receive his command at the time of passage. Saigo's request was denied, but the reply came too late. The Satsuma army of thirteen thousand marched forward anyway. Anticipating their arrival, the imperial army reinforced the castle with nearly forty-four hundred men and had more than thirteen thousand forces standing by. Nearly all imperial army soldiers were conscripts called up for duty by the young Meiji government.

The Satsuma Rebellion pitted a well-trained samurai army imbued deeply with traditional concepts of feudal Japan against an army of "conscripted farmers" with relatively little training. However, the imperial army had at its command all of the resources of the modernizing country, an unlimited supply of men and arms, and

Takehiko Ideishi, *The True Story of the Siege of Kumamoto Castle*, translated by James H. Buck. New York: Vantage Press, 1976. Copyright © 1976 by James H. Buck. All rights reserved. Reproduced by permission of the Literary Estate of James H. Buck.

more sophisticated weapons. Nevertheless, it took nearly seven
months to put down the Satsuma Rebellion. The imperial victory
proved that military insurrection could not reverse the policies of
the young Meiji government and freed the country to continue
unimpeded on the path of modernization.

When the rebel forces reached Kumamoto, the imperial army
commander refused their right of passage as expected. The Satsuma
rebels attacked the city and the imperial forces that had formed a
garrison inside the castle. The Kumamoto siege lasted fifty-four
days and was the final and definitive battle of the Satsuma Rebellion. Takehiko Ideishi was a lieutenant of artillery in the imperial
Japanese forces that formed the garrison at Kumamoto Castle. Fifty
years after the event, he recorded his experiences at the castle in a
series of three lectures, which were later translated by James H.
Buck. Ideishi provides valuable insights and details of the daily life
of the conscript army under attack by the last of the samurai forces.
The following essay is the third and final part of the story of the
siege at Kumamoto Castle in the spring of 1877 and marked the final military rebellion against the Meiji government.

Today, I shall speak about the great meeting engagement
which occurred soon after at Katayama Mansion and at
Tateyama. One might say this was the first great battle
fought during the siege of the [Kumamoto] castle.

This meeting engagement occurred on March 12 [1877]. The
Tateyama area was occupied by the [Satsuma] rebels, who were
concentrated there. Guards were stationed and waiting in the
Katayama area, the scene of frequent combat. When it became
night, none of us ventured out; however, the enemy sent out foot
patrols so that the friendly and enemy sides came even closer to
each other. From the other side, we were reviled by their yelling
to us, "I guess you're out of rice, aren't you?" From our side, we
answered such things as, "What a stupid thing to say! We aren't
men who live by eating sweet potatoes." We answered their
scolding by saying, "You must be out of ammunition. Shall we
see about that?" And while the two sides were in this kind of
confrontation, they sometimes even exchanged inquiries such as,
"Is so-and-so over there with you?"

As you know, this was a war in which older brother fought

younger brother and fathers and sons killed each other. There are true stories of times when relatives and friends crept close to each other at night and exchanged words. Nevertheless, there were also frequent exchanges such as, "Crazy fool! How did you ever turn into a rebel? Smell a skunk!" Sometimes small arms fire was exchanged and it ended with that.

Corpses Lay in Heaps

Well, on March 12, Police Inspector Ikebata went out of the castle in command of fourteen or fifteen police from the Metropolitan Police Unit—"Someway or other we'll punish those bastards." That was rough talk, but they approached closer and closer to the enemy. The battle was unexpected. Because the police unit advanced rapidly and approached to within 84–90 feet of the rebel firing positions, the enemy could not help but fire on them and the police could not withdraw. For our side, in order to protect the police by covering fire, we had no alternative but to attack fiercely. In no time at all, this action turned into a great battle. As long as the ammunition lasted, both sides incessantly made rash assaults against the other. That battle lasted two days and nights from the twelfth. Corpses lay in heaps on the battlefield. Blood flowed enough to make a river. In the end, victory was gained by the garrison troops. The enemy withdrew from Shubino and Tateyama. However, the losses were really great, and in this battle the defending forces had about eighty casualties. The enemy left seventy-three corpses. I don't know how many corpses they carried off to the rear. Later we buried these corpses nearby in a common grave and put up a grave marker reading "Grave of 73 Rebels." Even now the grave should still be there. It has become a remembrance which retains the tragedy and pathos of that year. . . .

After taking Tateyama by storm, the morale of the defending troops was unexpectedly enthusiastic. On the rebel side, their fantasy had been frustrated and they ceased immediately to attack. More and more, they adopted a stratagem of waiting. More and more, it became a matter for them of surrounding the castle at a distance. Then began the famous plan for the flooding of Kumamoto Castle (*mizuzeme*) and the dispositions of the opposing troops changed into an old-fashioned battle array. . . .

The most important thing that happened was the insufficiency of food provisions within the castle, which got worse day by day.

Already, the situation was extremely serious. Although we had been under siege for only a short time, it now was a situation where something like death by starvation could happen. The stout soldiers had their ration reduced from three meals a day to two meals a day. This perhaps was a risk to life, but the most heartless aspect was the lack of food such as should be fed to the sick and wounded. . . .

Relief from Boredom

Now, a few words about how the castle soldiers provided for their recreation. By this time, the garrison had gradually become accustomed to the war. As far as the army was concerned, they came to be somewhat indolent and bored. As I mentioned earlier in the example of the "war of words," the soldiers never lost, but one can't do that sort of thing forever. In time, they wearied even of this, and many different means and methods were devised for their entertainment. By this, I do not mean something thought up especially by the officers. After all, soldiers will be soldiers. We officers gave our greatest concern to the preservation of the soldiers' health and the encouragement of the martial spirit.

But these men were conscripts and among such a large number of soldiers there were some really sly characters, some talented performers. They put on vaudeville skits *(yose)* or variety entertainments quite often. Of course, this was not for the purpose of making money; it was just that a few men who were proud of their voices gathered together and put on the shows. At night they would put up a tent or a booth in the barracks or in the firing positions and here and there one would hear voices calling "Welcome! Step on up for the show!" If one went to take a look, he would see a stage had been built one level above the ground and a curtain would be hanging down in the form of a bamboo screen. Below the stage there was a large number of soldiers. Finally, from behind the scenes came the clacking of the wooden blocks of the musicians. The curtain was rolled up. It was an interesting thing to see. By some contrivance or other, there was even a *samisen* (a stringed instrument). The master-of-ceremonies was wearing a paper *kamishimo* (an old ceremonial dress) over his military uniform. He lowered his head and in a rhythmic voice he began his announcements, "Hear Ye! Hear Ye! Ladies and Gentlemen! I have the pleasure to announce the presentation of the *joruri* (ballad-drama) titled . . ." and so forth. We were waiting. Then the audience was everywhere shouting, "Master-of-ceremonies! Do a good job for us. Let's hear it!" As soon as the recitation was finished, the drums played. A story began, then a magician took over the stage . . . there were all kinds of excitement and tumult.

They did this sort of thing every evening, every night. It relieved the ennui of the daytime and built up morale. Later I heard that the rebel troops heard the sounds of the strings *(samisen)* and thought we had brought *geisha* into the castle and were enjoying ourselves with them. The enemy were very angry, or so I heard. . . .

More Fighting Around the Castle

On March 26, there was heard the sound of artillery fire in the area of Matsubashi on the Kagoshima road to the east of Kumamoto Castle. This signalled contact between Major General Yamada's Independent Brigade and the rebels, but we didn't learn this until later. Well, the war had broken out in this area, too, we thought, and on the twenty-seventh combat in this area became more and more intense. Now we were in the midst of war. What we wanted most was to destroy the rebels and quickly press out of the castle-city. Everyone was privately praying to his own Shinto god or to Buddha. On the twenty-eighth, a secret messenger sneaked into the castle from the brigade headquarters at Ueki-guchi. This fellow was named Fukuda Johei and he was a native of Ueki. With painstaking effort, he had avoided the rebel encirclement and finally arrived at the castle. Prior to his departure from the brigade, any number of men had been dispatched but not a single one had succeeded. Fukuda was the first to make it. He reported that the confrontation of the two armies at Yamaka-guchi extended for a distance of about seventeen miles. Minami-no-seki (the Imperial Forces) had seized Mukozaka and advanced as far as Kidome.

The inspection within the castle on March 1 had shown that food supplies were adequate to last only nineteen days. Now we were already into the last ten days of March and by all sorts of stratagems we had been able to keep body and soul together. But the future was dark. All we heard was "Friendly troops are coming. Friendly troops are coming," but once again not a shadow nor a trace of them could be seen. . . .

We waited. "Will it be today? Or tomorrow?" Although we managed to exist, there was still no messenger. As the war became more intense on all sides, hope within the castle gradually dwindled. Provisions became more and more scarce. Regardless of what we might do in the future, it became ever more evident how thin was the thread of life of the 4,000 men in the besieged castle. There seems to be no figure of speech adequate to describe the sense of helplessness. In order to try to preserve the castle for one more day at a time, we tried to devise a scheme for the provisions, but, since nothing could be done about their supply, we had to plan to limit the individual intake and thus stretch the food supplies to last into the future. So we rationed the food. . . .

Breaking the Rebel Encirclement

Now, a few remarks about the plans to break the encirclement from inside the castle. In the midst of the hustle and bustle of men and animals, time passed. It was now the third lunar month. Although there were cherry trees, they did not bloom. Birds sang, but there was no tone quality. The longed-for spring haze seemed to be battle smoke. Like a dream, March had departed. Finally, it was April 1. Checking into the supply of provisions, it was estimated that it would last twelve to thirteen days into the future if we adulterated the millet. Up to this time, only combatants had been fed boiled rice, but this seemed to be a dangerous practice. So it was decided to feed boiled millet to everyone inside the castle. No matter how much we wanted to feed boiled rice, we could not do so. Things got to the point where we had exhausted all of our stratagems. Our fate was entrusted to Heaven, and we awaited the reinforcing troops. . . .

Truly, the castle soldiers were starving to death with no regrets. The garrison would be slaughtered before the reinforcing troops could arrive. This was a matter to which one would swear before all the gods of heaven and earth—one which could not be endured. But what could be done? No plan had been worked out inside the castle. Being pressed so closely, in the end it was decided—repressing one's tears—that the only measure left was to organize and deploy the so-called break-out unit.

To die and save how many thousands of troops within the castle? To live to welcome the arrival of the rescuing troops? One of these two courses of action had to be selected. On this occasion, the plan was to try to penetrate the rebels' close investment by a bold action just before dawn on April 8. . . . On April 7, a fragmentary plan for the break-out was provided each individual. This had been drafted at great pains by Commanding General Tani, whose blood and tears were in every word. The text read:

> For more than forty days we have awaited the raid by the Shigiko Brigade into the castle. However, even now we hear only the sound of artillery fire and not a single man has entered Kumamoto. In view of the foregoing, and in order to plan for the future, we can not expect assistance within the next several days. Therefore, to preserve the remaining provisions, it is necessary to decide on a charge against the enemy. I desire the break-out to take place on the eighth. The method is described generally below:

> To: 1st Unit, 2nd Unit, etc.

> This one battle will be the crossroads of life for the entire garrison The break-out troops must disregard their own casualties, disregard rebels located on other routes of advance, advance straight ahead [and so forth]. . . .

> Because the fate of this Castle is at stake, Tateki himself will be at the head of the troops and shall command them. Both Karayama and Kodama are requested to provide for the sick and to look after things after my death. . . .

It was decided to penetrate the enemy's close siege of the castle on April 8, to find one single straight route out of the castle and advance along this one route. It was now dusk on the seventh and there was nothing to do but wait for dawn of the eighth. . . .

On the previous night, the direction of penetration through the enemy siege was to have been in the direction of Ueki, but from the evening of the seventh onward, the fighting had become more intense in what was apparently the Kawashiri-guchi area. About midnight on the seventh, the plan was suddenly changed. For the soldiers making the sortie from the castle, it was the once-in-a-lifetime occurrence and for those staying in the castle it was to be the one great battle to determine the fate of the garrison. Reflecting on these matters, we did not want to give soldiers the daily diet of millet gruel. . . . There was the idea that if the rebels carried the garrison and looked around after they had killed us, they would laugh at us and say, "Hey. Look here! The castle soldiers were eating millet." This was something which did not amuse the soldier going out to meet death, nor did it appeal to those who would stay behind. So, regardless of how low the supplies were within the castle, we decided to give rice to every member of the break-out unit—and vegetables, too. Horses were of greatest importance to us, but we butchered three of them and had the soldiers carry the meat with them. The break-out unit had the mission to move out through the mist of dawn, leave the castle, first penetrate the encirclement in the Ansei Bridge area, and link up with the reinforcing troops at Kawashiri. The advance party, in hushed silence, was passed out through the castle gate. These officers and men regretfully were to sacrifice themselves for the garrison. Slowly, they advanced toward the jaws of death. . . .

The time was 4 A.M. on April 8, 1877. The penetration unit in the vanguard was followed silently out of the castle gate by the main body of the break-out unit. This was their farewell look at Kumamoto Castle. It was pitch-dark and the castle donjon towered beautifully against the starlight in the background. The break-out unit's route of advance was first from the Hirai Road to Ansei Bridge, there to ford the Shira River, enter Suizen Temple, and to proceed along the Mifune Highway heading toward the battle area of Kawashiri. It was to be a straight route. The penetration unit which led this column was intended to attack the rebel positions between Ansei Bridge and Myogo Bridge, concealing themselves as much as possible during a secret approach. . . .

The Break-Out Unit Returns

Before dawn on the morning of April 14, we were in the midst of combat on all sides. The combat in the Kawashiri area was extraordinarily violent from about 6:00 A.M., and even this battle increased in intensity. Even in the castle, guns were being fired with reckless abandon and we tried to encourage them with shouts but, after all, it seemed like the battle went on without change. The fighting ended in the afternoon. This was, indeed, very strange, and we were unable to console ourselves with any good thoughts. We suffered, each in our private way, wondering whether our side had been defeated, and we were anxious about the whereabouts of our comrades. Suddenly, about 4:00 P.M., carbine fire broke out very close to the garrison. At the same time, a military unit was pushing close to Choroku Bridge, cool as a cucumber. We didn't know if the unit were enemy or friendly. If they were enemy, we could not let them get away. If they were friendly, we would have to provide appropriate assistance. We felt we should not interfere recklessly. They continued to come toward us. The attire of the point formation was uniform. Among them, the leader was waving a hand flag. He continued to approach. He arrived at Yamazaki Parade Ground. Then for the first time we got a close look at the main body. Would you believe it? This was the messenger from Heaven to Kumamoto Castle: it was the rescue Independent Brigade for which we had waited so long. They had splendidly destroyed the enemy at Kawashiri-guchi and with great prowess and courage had arrived safely below the castle. I really can't describe the gleeful shouts and the jumping for joy. The commander of the advance guard was then–Lieutenant Colonel Yamakawa Hiroshi. As he came up to the dismount bridge, he cried loudly, "We've come. We're here! We've driven all those fellows out of Kawashiri-guchi." There was tremendous tumult. Inside the castle, regardless of what one might say, it was the greatest, most boisterous day since the first ten days of February. At last—until this very day—we had been in seclusion in the isolated castle. Now the Will of Heaven unfolded in our favor and once again we could see the light of the sun. That is to say, it was dusk on April 14. Cheers of joy shook heaven and earth. The break-out unit returned to Kumamoto Castle at 4:00 P.M. on April 15. They had returned with their dead and the tears could not be stopped. Link-up was also made this day with the Imperial Army at Ueki-guchi, and those units also entered the castle. With this, I conclude my remarks on the Siege of Kumamoto Castle.

Medicine, Public Health, and the Germ Theory

by René Dubos

René Dubos, was a Pulitzer Prize–winning microbiologist, professor, and author of many books, articles, and essays. In his lifetime, he did a great deal of research on tuberculosis as well as ecological applications of microbiology. Many fundamental principles of sustainable ecology stem from Dubos's work and research. He was also very interested in the social applications of medicine and germ theory and had a particular interest in the work of Louis Pasteur.

In this essay, Dubos describes the various applications that have been made using Pasteur's germ theory of disease. He also describes how the discovery that most disease is caused by microorganisms has changed not only the science of medicine but also the way medicine is practiced. The practice of modern medicine has its roots in two ancient Greek systems. The first school is the Hippocratic method, and it originates in Cos, Greece. Medicine in Cos was concerned with the patient rather than the disease and considered the environment of decisive importance in conditioning the behavior and performance of the body. The second, based in Cnidus, was based on the diagnosis of different diseases and the attempt to classify and describe them as separate entities. Dubos describes how the bacteriological era represents the fruition of this ancient biology.

Since the discovery of the germ theory, the pendulum has swung widely in both directions. Ultimately, modern medicine constitutes a

René Dubos, *Louis Pasteur: Free Lance of Science*. New York: Charles Scribner's Sons, 1976.
Copyright © 1950 by René J. Dubos. All rights reserved. Reproduced by permission of The Gale Group.

balance of both approaches. Most importantly, knowledge of the existence of microbial agents has made it possible to learn more about the fundamental processes of the human body and has provided the basis for the treatment of disease and prolonging human life.

The germ theory of disease constitutes one of the most important milestones in the evolution of medicine. It dispelled some of the mystery and much of the terror of contagion; it facilitated and rendered more precise the diagnosis of disease; it provided a rational basis for the development of prophylactic and therapeutic procedures. These great achievements should not lead one to assume that progress in the control of infectious disease dates from the bacteriological era. In reality, many of the most devastating scourges have been conquered without the benefit of laboratory research, and some have even disappeared without any conscious effort on the part of man.

In the course of recorded history, overwhelming epidemics have arrested invading armies on the march, decimated populations, disorganized the social fabric, changed the pattern of civilizations—but mankind has survived. Life has proved flexible enough to triumph over yellow fever, influenza, typhus, plague, cholera, syphilis, malaria, even when there were available no effective measures to combat disease. Less dramatic, but fully as astonishing as the spontaneous and often sudden termination of the great epidemics, is the continuous downward trend of certain diseases in the course of centuries. . . .

Application of the Germ Theory

The germ theory led to a more accurate understanding of the circumstances under which host and parasite come into contact, and thus permitted the formulation of rational control policies of greater effectiveness than those devised empirically in the past. Knowledge of the properties and behavior of the infective microorganism often suggested means to attack it, either before or after it had reached the human body. Such is the practice of immunization—which consists in establishing a specific resistance against a given contagious disease by exposing the body, under very special conditions, to the infective agent, to an attenuated form of it, or to one of its products. The science of immunity is one of the most direct outcomes of the germ theory; and it is the more surprising, therefore, to realize that immunization had been practiced during antiquity, long before anything was known of the role of microorganisms as agents of disease; vaccination against "Oriental sore" and against smallpox are among the most successful and ancient achievements of preventive medicine. . . .

Surgical Practice Improved

In the past, infections had always been the chief cause of the mortality following operations of any sort. Of the 13,000 amputations performed in the French Army during the Franco-Prussian War in 1870–1871, no less than 10,000 proved fatal. Here and there, individual surgeons attempted to lessen mortality by cleanliness and by the employment of special washes for wounds, but all these attempts were empirical and in general did not avail. It was [Louis] Pasteur's demonstration that bacteria were responsible for fermentations and putrefactions which gave the clue that [English surgeon and scientist Joseph] Lister followed to reform surgical practice.

Lister's attention was called to Pasteur's work on the role of microorganisms in putrefaction sometime around 1864, by the chemist [Thomas] Anderson. He was well prepared to understand the significance of Pasteur's observations because . . . his father had early made him familiar with the microbial world. If, as Lister postulated, microorganisms cause wound suppuration, just as they cause fermentation and putrefaction, they must be excluded at all costs from the hands of the surgeon, from his instruments, and from the very air surrounding the operating field. To achieve this Lister used a spray of phenol throughout the operations, taking his lead from the fact that this substance was then employed for the disinfection of sewage and excreta. Within a short time, he acquired the conviction that his antiseptic technique prevented suppuration and permitted healing "by first intention" in the majority of cases.

This antiseptic method was based on the hypothesis, derived from Pasteur's writings in the 1860's, that wound contamination originated chiefly from microorganisms present in the air. As he began to frequent hospital wards, however, Pasteur became more and more convinced that the importance of the air-borne microorganisms had been exaggerated and that the most important conveyors of infection were the persons who took care of the sick. He emphasized this point of view in a famous lecture delivered before the Academy of Medicine.

"This water, this sponge, this lint with which you wash or cover a wound, deposit germs which have the power of multiplying rapidly within the tissues and which would invariably cause the death of the patient in a very short time, if the vital processes of the body did not counteract them. But alas, the vital resistance is too often impotent; too often the constitution of the wounded, his weakness, his morale, and the inadequate dressing of the wound, oppose an insufficient barrier to the invasion of these infinitely small organisms that, unwittingly, you have introduced into the injured part. If I had the honor of being a surgeon, impressed as I am with the dangers to which the patient is exposed by the microbes present over the surface of all objects, particularly in hospitals, not only would I use none but perfectly clean instruments, but after having cleansed my hands with the greatest care, and subjected them to a rapid flaming, which would expose them to no more inconvenience than that felt by a smoker who passes a glowing coal from one hand to the other, I would use only lint, bandages and sponges previously exposed to a temperature of 130° to 150° C."

This memorable statement has become the basis of aseptic surgery, which aims at preventing access of pathogenic agents to the operative field rather than trying to kill them with antiseptics applied to the tissues.

A New World of Germs

One might think that, by 1878, the germ theory would be sufficiently well-established to make Pasteur's warnings needless. In reality, the sense of aseptic technique was still at that time completely foreign to many enlightened physicians, as is revealed by the following account . . . : "One day, at the Hôtel Dieu, Professor Richet was asked by Pasteur to collect pus from one of the surgical cases. He was doing his ward rounds with a soiled white apron over his black dress suit. Interrupting himself, he said, 'We are going to open this abscess; bring me the small alcohol lamp which M. Pasteur used yesterday to flame the tube in which he collected some pus for his experiment. We shall now sacrifice to the new fashion and flame the scalpel,' and with a wide gesture, which was characteristic of him, he wiped the scalpel on the soiled apron twice, and then attacked the abscess."

In contrast to the carelessness of his medical colleagues, Pasteur carried his concern for aseptic precautions to the most extreme degree. The odd advice to the surgeons that they flame their hands before operating on their patients reflected a procedure which was part of routine technique in his laboratory until 1886. Pasteur's habit of cleaning glasses, plates and silverware with his napkin before every meal is easier to understand when placed in the atmosphere created by the recent discovery of disease germs. He had shown that the *vibrion septique*, commonly present in the intestinal content of animals and in soil, could also be the cause of violent death if it reached susceptible tissues. He had seen in the blood and organs of women dying of childbirth fever a streptococcus which was similar in appearance to that found in many fermenting fluids. In this bewildering new world which unfolded before him, there were at first no criteria to judge where danger might be lurking. True enough, he was aware of the fact that in addition to the dangerous microorganisms, there are many which are completely innocuous, but as no techniques were then available to differentiate the black sheep from the white, he deemed it advisable to exert the utmost caution in everyday life. . . .

The Philosophy of Healing

Pasteur never took an active part in the formulation of public health regulations; he left to others the duty to administer the land which he had conquered. Chemotherapy—that is, the treatment of established disease by the use of drugs—is another field of medical microbiology which he did not till. He had not ignored it, but he did not believe that it was the most useful approach to the control of infection. "When meditating over a disease, I never think of finding a remedy for it, but, instead, a means of preventing it." This is a policy which enlightened societies are slowly learning to adopt, one which the wise men of China have understood—if it be true that they advise paying doctors to prevent sickness, rather than to treat it. It is also possible that Pasteur was kept from working on chemotherapy by another reason that appears as a casual sentence in one of his reports on the silkworm diseases:

"My experiments (on silkworms) have brought the knowledge of the prevailing diseases to a point where one could approach scientifically the search for a remedy. . . . However, discoveries of this nature are more the result of chance than of reasoned orderly studies.". . .

Accidents Are Sometimes Important Discoveries

It is one of Pasteur's own accidental observations which ushered in the most spectacular phase of discoveries in the field of therapy of infectious disease. He had observed that cultures of anthrax bacilli contaminated with common bacteria often lose their ability to establish disease in experimental animals, and he rightly concluded that these common bacteria produced some substance inimical to the disease agent. Was it sheer luck, or the desire to comment on this interesting phenomenon, or real vision, that inspired him to predict a great future for his chance observation? "Neutral or slightly alkaline urine is an excellent medium for the bacilli [of anthrax]. . . . But if . . . one of the common aerobic microorganisms is sown at the same time, the anthrax bacilli grow only poorly and die out sooner or later. It is a remarkable thing that the same phenomenon is seen in the body even of those animals most susceptible to anthrax, leading to the astonishing result that anthrax bacilli can be introduced in profusion into an animal, which yet does not develop the disease. . . . These facts perhaps justify the highest hopes for therapeutics."

The hint was not lost. Immediately after him, and ever since, many bacteriologists have attempted to find in nature microorganisms capable of producing substances effective in the treatment of infectious disease. The story of this search does not belong here. The title of its most important chapter, "Penicillin," is sufficient to call to mind the accidental detection of a mold which inhibited the growth of staphylococcus, and then the organized effort of pathologists, bacteriologists, chemists and technologists to make the miraculous drug available to the world. Initially, it was a chance observation which revealed the existence of penicillin; but again it was true that "chance favors only the prepared mind." In this case, the mind favored by chance had been prepared by years of familiarity with bacteriological lore. Not only did the germ theory permit the discovery of penicillin; it also guided at every step those who worked to define the immense possibilities of the drug in the treatment of disease. Today, it still guides the search for other substances capable of interfering with the pathogenic behavior of the microbial agents of infection. . . .

A few attempts, patterned after Pasteur's experiments on the effect of chicken cholera on rabbits, have since been made to control animal and plant plagues by the use of other microbial parasites. Best known are those utilizing bacteria pathogenic for rats and mice, and also for certain plant pests. Although encouraging results have been obtained, they have not lived up to the early expectations. It is relatively easy to cause the death of animals with infected food, but it is extremely difficult to establish an epidemic with a progressive course. A few years ago, an attempt was made in Australia to introduce the virus of infectious myxomatosis on an island infested with rabbits. In this case again, the disease did not become established in the rabbit pop-

Louis Pasteur's germ theory changed the way medicine was practiced and led to the discovery of life-saving vaccines.

ulation although myxomatosis is known to be a highly fatal disease for these animals. As pointed out repeatedly in preceding pages, the spread of any infection is conditioned by a multitude of factors, many of them unknown; epidemics often break out in a mysterious manner, but they also subside spontaneously for equally obscure reasons. If this were not the case, leprosy, tuberculosis, plague, cholera, typhus, influenza, poliomyelitis and countless other scourges would have long ago annihilated the human race. The factors which limit the spread of epidemics have been responsible so far for the failure of the microbiological warfare devised by Pasteur to control animal plagues. Fortunately they limit also the destructive potentialities of microbiological warfare between men, at least until more knowledge is available.

There is a tragic irony in the fact that one of the last of Pasteur's experimental studies should have been devoted to the utilization of a technique by which contagious disease can be used to destroy life. Today, further progress in the control of infection depends to a large extent upon a more thorough understanding of the factors which govern the spread of epidemics and it is this very knowledge which is also needed to make of biological warfare the self-reproducing weapon of future wars. This prospect, however, should not be held as an argument to minimize the beneficial results of microbiological sciences. For, as [English philosopher] Francis Bacon said, "If the debasement of arts and sciences to purposes of wickedness, luxury, and the like, be made a ground of objection, let no one be moved thereby. For the same may be said of all earthly goods; of wit, courage, strength, beauty, wealth, light itself, and the rest.". . .

After 1877, . . . physicians, as well as the lay public, became obsessed with the thought of disease germs. Today, many medical scholars lament the fact that, under the influence of the germ theory, too much emphasis has been placed on the microorganisms which cause disease, and too little on the effects exerted by hereditary constitution, climate, season and nutritional state on susceptibility to infection. In this justified criticism there is often implied the belief that Pasteur, who was not a physician, was responsible for a distortion of medical thinking. In reality, the complete sacrifice of the physiological to the bacteriological point of view is not Pasteur's guilt but that of the medical bacteriologists who followed him during the so-called "Golden era of bacteriology." True enough, Pasteur had to limit his own experimental work to the study of microorganisms and of their activities, but this limitation was the consequence of the shortness of days and of life, and not of the narrowness of his concepts. On many occasions, he referred to the importance of constitution and environment for the occurrence of disease, and to his desire to investigate them. Unfortunately, he was prevented from doing it by the fierceness of the controversies concerning the participation of microorganisms in disease, and by the enormous amount of experimental work required to bring unassailable proof of his views. This effort monopolized all his energies, even though it did not satisfy his genius. . . .

The Evolution of Medicine

Many needful discoveries remain to be made before the role of microorganisms in disease is completely known and controlled; the Pasteurian chapter is not closed, and will never be forgotten. But acceptance of the germ theory of disease was only one step in the evolution of medicine. Knowledge of the existence and properties of the microbial parasites is making it easier to study the fundamental processes of the living body, its intrinsic strength and weaknesses, its reaction to the environment. Medicine can again become Hippocratic now that contagion is no longer a mysterious and unpredictable threat to the life of man. Thanks to the germ theory, it has become possible to analyze with greater profit the part played by nature and nurture in health and in disease, as well as the pervasive influence of "Air, Water and Places."

Louis Pasteur's Germ Theory of Disease Transforms Public Health: 1877

The Germ Theory and Its Applications to Medicine and Surgery

by Louis Pasteur

Louis Pasteur undoubtedly made some of the most important contributions to medicine and microbiology. His discovery that most infectious diseases are caused by germs is known as the germ theory of disease. This discovery is one of the most important in medical history. His discoveries and their applications led to life-changing practices in medicine, farming, industry, and public health. The method of destroying harmful microbes in perishable food products by using heat is known as pasteurization. His germ theory led to the development of life-saving vaccines and the discovery of viruses. He championed changes in hospital practices and surgery to minimize the spread of disease by microbes. He also described the scientific basis for fermentation, wine making, and the brewing of beer. Pasteur's work gave birth to many branches of science, and he was single-handedly responsible for some of the most important theoretical concepts and practical applications of modern science.

By identifying individual microbes that were present in the hu-

Louis Pasteur, *Scientific Papers*, vol. 38, part 7. New York: Collier & Son, 1909–1914.

man body during illness, Pasteur was able to formulate a means of protecting people against the hazards of both germs and viruses. Pasteur is credited with pinpointing the cause of many contagious diseases of the late 1800s and then developing vaccines to treat and prevent them. Out of Pasteur's conclusions and data would come vaccinations for diphtheria, tetanus, anthrax, chicken cholera, silk-worm disease, tuberculosis, and the dreaded plague.

Louis Pasteur was born in 1822 in Jura, France. The International Pasteur Institutes continue his work today. The institutes are some of the world's leading research institutes and employ a world-renowned international staff of scientists and physicians. A teaching hospital at the institutes specializes in infectious and immune dis-eases, closely working with AIDS and cancer patients to devise new ways of aggressively treating and preventing disease. The Graduate Study Center and Epidemiological Screening Unit strive to identify new microorganisms and develop ways to treat them.

The following paper was delivered by Louis Pasteur at the French Academy of Sciences on April 29, 1878. He outlines the principles of the germ theory and its applications to medicine and surgery.

The Sciences gain by mutual support. When, as the result of my first communications on the fermentations in 1857–1858, it appeared that the ferments, properly so-called, are living beings, that the germs of microscopic organisms abound in the surface of all objects, in the air and in water; that the the-ory of spontaneous generation is chimerical; that wines, beer, vinegar, the blood, urine and all the fluids of the body undergo none of their usual changes in pure air, both Medicine and Surgery received fresh stimulation. A French physician, Dr. Davaine, was fortunate in making the first application of these principles to Medicine, in 1863.

Anthrax Is a Bacterial Disease

Our researches of last year [1877] left the eurology of the putrid disease, or septicemia, in a much less advanced condition than that of anthrax. We had demonstrated the probability that septicemia depends upon the presence and growth of a microscopic body, but the absolute proof of this important conclusion was not reached.

To demonstrate experimentally that a microscopic organism actually is the cause of a disease and the agent of contagion, I know no other way, in the present state of Science, than to subject the *microbe* (the new and happy term introduced by M. Sedillot) to the method of cultivation out of the body. It may be noted that in twelve successive cultures, each one of only ten cubic centimeters volume, the original drop will be diluted as if placed in a volume of fluid equal to the total volume of the earth. It is just this form of test to which M. Joubert and I subjected the anthrax bacteridium. Having cultivated it a great number of times in a sterile fluid, each culture being started with a minute drop from the preceding, we then demonstrated that the product of the last culture was capable of further development and of acting in the animal tissues by producing anthrax with all its symptoms. Such is—as we believe—the indisputable proof that *anthrax is a bacterial disease.*

A New Difficulty

Our researches concerning the septic vibrio [bacteria] had not so far been convincing, and it was to fill up this gap that we resumed our experiments. To this end, we attempted the cultivation of the septic vibrio from an animal dead of septicemia. It is worth noting that all of our first experiments failed, despite the variety of culture media we employed—urine, beer yeast water, meat water, etc. Our culture media were not sterile, but we found—most commonly—a microscopic organism showing no relationship to the septic vibrio, and presenting the form, common enough elsewhere, of chains of extremely minute spherical granules possessed of no virulence whatever. This was an impurity, introduced, unknown to us, at the same time as the septic vibrio; and the germ undoubtedly passed from the intestines—always inflamed and distended in septicemic animals—into the abdominal fluids from which we took our original cultures of the septic vibrio. If this explanation of the contamination of our cultures was correct, we ought to find a pure culture of the septic vibrio in the heart's blood of an animal recently dead of septicemia. This was what happened, but a new difficulty presented itself; all our cultures remained sterile. Furthermore this sterility was accompanied by loss in the culture media of (the original) virulence.

It occurred to us that septic vibrio might be an obligatory anaërobe and that the sterility of our inoculated culture fluids might be due to the destruction of the septic vibrio by the atmospheric oxygen dissolved in the fluids. The Academy may remember that I have previously demonstrated facts of this nature in regard to the vibrio of butyric fermentation, which not only lives without air but is killed by the air.

It was necessary therefore to attempt to cultivate the septic vibrio either in a vacuum or in the presence of inert gases—such as carbonic acid.

Results justified our attempt, the septic vibrio grew easily in a complete vacuum, and no less easily in the presence of pure carbonic acid.

Proof That Oxygen Destroys Germs

These results have a necessary corollary. If a fluid containing septic vibrios be exposed to pure air, the vibrios should be killed and all virulence should disappear. This is actually the case. If some drops of septic serum be spread horizontally in a tube and in a very thin layer, the fluid will become absolutely harmless in less than half a day, even if at first it was so virulent as to produce death upon the inoculation of the smallest portion of a drop.

Furthermore all the vibrios, which crowded the liquid as motile threads, are destroyed and disappear. After the action of the air, only fine amorphous granules can be found, unfit for culture as well as for the transmission of any disease whatever. It might be said that the air burned the vibrios.

If it is a terrifying thought that life is at the mercy of the multiplication of these minute bodies, it is a consoling hope that Science will not always remain powerless before such enemies, since for example at the very beginning of the study we find that simple exposure to air is sufficient at times to destroy them.

Germs Can Protect Themselves

But, if oxygen destroys the vibrios, how can septicemia exist, since atmospheric air is present everywhere? How can such facts be brought in accord with the germ theory? How can blood, exposed to air, become septic through the dust the air contains?

All things are hidden, obscure and debatable if the cause of the phenomena be unknown, but everything is clear if this cause be known. What we have just said is true only of a septic fluid containing adult vibrios, in active development by fission: conditions are different when the vibrios are transformed into their germs, that is into the glistening corpuscles first described and figured in my studies on silk-worm disease, in dealing with worms dead of the disease called "flachérie." Only the adult vibrios disappear, burn up, and lose their virulence in contact with air: the germ corpuscles, under these conditions, remain always ready for new cultures, and for new inoculations.

All this however does not do away with the difficulty of understanding how septic germs can exist on the surface of objects, floating in the air and in water.

Where can these corpuscles originate? Nothing is easier than the production of these germs, in spite of the presence of air in contact with septic fluids.

If abdominal serous exudate containing septic vibrios actively growing by fission be exposed to the air, as we suggested above, but with the precaution of giving a substantial thickness to the layer, even if only one centimeter be used, this curious phenomenon will appear in a few hours. The oxygen is absorbed in the upper layers of the fluid—as is indicated by the change of color. Here the vibrios are dead and disappear. In the deeper layers, on the other hand, towards the bottom of this centimeter of septic fluid we suppose to be under observation, the vibros continue to multiply by fission—protected from the action of oxygen by those that have perished above them: little by little they pass over to the condition of germ corpuscles with the gradual disappearance of the thread forms. So that instead of moving threads of varying length, sometimes greater than the field of the microscope, there is to be seen only a number of glittering points, lying free or surrounded by a scarcely perceptible amorphous mass. Thus is formed, containing the latent germ life, no longer in danger from the destructive action of oxygen, thus, I repeat, is formed the septic dust, and we are able to understand what has before seemed so obscure, we can see how putrescible fluids can be inoculated by the dust of the air, and how it is that putrid diseases are permanent in the world.

An Entirely New Field

The Academy will permit me, before leaving these interesting results, to refer to one of their main theoretical consequences. At the very beginning of these researches, for they reveal an entirely new field, what must be insistently demanded? The absolute proof that there actually exist transmissible, contagious, infectious diseases of which the cause lies essentially and solely in the presence of microscopic organisms. The proof that for at least some diseases, the conception of spontaneous virulence must be for-ever abandoned—as well as the idea of contagion and an infec-tious element suddenly originating in the bodies of men or ani-mals and able to originate diseases which propagate themselves under identical forms: and all of those opinions fatal to medical progress, which have given rise to the gratuitous hypotheses of spontaneous generation, of albuminoid ferments, of hemiorgan-isms, of archebiosis, and many other conceptions without the least basis in observation. What is to be sought for in this instance is the proof that along with our vibrio there does not exist an inde-pendent virulence belonging to the surrounding fluids or solids, in short that the vibrio is not merely an epiphenomenon of the dis-ease of which it is the obligatory accompaniment. What then do we see, in the results that I have just brought out? A septic fluid, taken at the moment that the vibrios are not yet changed into germs, loses its virulence completely upon simple exposure to the air, but preserves this virulence, although exposed to air on the simple condition of being in a thick layer for some hours. In the first case, the virulence once lost by exposure to air, the liquid is incapable of taking it on again upon cultivation: but, in the sec-ond case, it preserves its virulence and can propagate, even after exposure to air. It is impossible, then, to assert that there is a sep-arate virulent substance, either fluid or solid, existing, apart from the adult vibrio or its germ. Nor can it be supposed that there is a virus which loses its virulence at the moment that the adult vib-rio dies; for such a substance should also lose its virulence when the vibrios, changed to germs, are exposed to the air. Since the virulence persists under these conditions it can only be due to the germ corpuscles—the only thing present. There is only one pos-sible hypothesis as to the existence of a virus in solution, and that is that such a substance, which was present in our experiment in non-fatal amounts, should be continuously furnished by the vib-rio itself, during its growth in the body of the living animal. But it is of little importance since the hypothesis supposes the form-ing and necessary existence of the vibrio.

Aërobic Microbes

I hasten to touch upon another series of observations which are even more deserving the attention of the surgeon than the preced-ing: I desire to speak of the effects of our microbe of pus when as-sociated with the septic vibrio. There is nothing more easy to superpose—as it were—two distinct diseases and to produce what might be called a *septicemic purulent infection*, or a *purulent septicemia*. Whilst the microbe-producing pus, when acting alone, gives rise to a thick pus, white, or sometimes with a yellow or bluish tint, not putrid, diffused or enclosed by the so-called *pyogenic membrane*, not dangerous, especially if localized in cellular tissue, ready, if the expression may be used for rapid resorption; on the other hand the smallest abscess produced by this organism when associated with the septic vibrio takes on a thick gangrenous appearance, putrid, greenish and infiltrating the softened tissues. In this case the microbe of pus carried so to speak by the septic vibrio, accompanies it throughout the body: the highly-inflamed muscular tissues, full of serous fluid, showing also globules of pus here and there, are like a kneading of the two organisms.

By a similar procedure the effects of the anthrax bacteridium and the microbe of pus may be combined and the two diseases may be superposed, so as to obtain a purulent anthrax or an anthracoid purulent infection. Care must be taken not to exaggerate the predominance of the new microbe over the bacteridium. If the microbe be associated with the latter in sufficient amount it may crowd it out completely—prevent it from growing in the body at all. Anthrax does not appear, and the infection, entirely local, becomes merely an abscess whose cure is easy. The microbe-producing pus and the septic vibrio (not) being both anaërobes, as we have demonstrated it is evident that the latter will not much disturb its neighbor. Nutrient substances, fluid or solid, can scarcely be deficient in the tissues from such minute organisms. But the anthrax bacteridium is exclusively aërobic, and the proportion of oxygen is far from being equally distributed throughout the tissues: innumerable conditions can diminish or exhaust the supply here and there, and since the microbe-producing pus is also aërobic, it can be understood how, by using a quantity slightly greater than that of the bacteridium it might easily deprive the latter of the oxygen necessary for it. But the explanation of the fact is of little importance: it is certain that under some conditions the microbe we are speaking of entirely prevents the development of the bacteridium.

New Practices in Surgery

Summarizing—it appears from the preceding facts that it is possible to produce at will, purulent infections with no elements of putrescence, putrescent purulent infections, anthracoid purulent infections, and finally combinations of these types of lesions varying according to the proportions of the mixtures of the specific organisms made to act on the living tissues.

These are the principal facts I have to communicate to the Academy in my name and in the names of my collaborators, Messrs. Joubert and Chamberland. Some weeks ago (Session of the 11th of March last) a member of the Section of Medicine and Surgery, M. Sedillot, after long meditation on the lessons of a brilliant career, did not hesitate to assert that the successes as well as the failures of Surgery find a rational explanation in the principles upon which the germ theory is based, and that this theory would found a new Surgery—already begun by a celebrated English surgeon, Dr. [Joseph] Lister, who was among the first to understand its fertility. With no professional authority, but with the conviction of a trained experimenter, I venture here to repeat the words of an eminent *confrère.*

10

Queen Victoria Is Made Empress of India: 1877

The End of Empire

by David Gilmour

In 1877 the prime minister of England, Benjamin Disraeli, appointed Queen Victoria empress of India. Although Victoria never visited India, she took a personal interest in the country, and it was following her suggestion that the appointment was made. Until the great mutiny and civil rebellion of 1857, India was not directly ruled by the British Crown but by the English East India Company, which was a chartered monopoly corporation beholden to its directors and shareholders. By the 1840s the British East India Company had brought almost all of India under British control, and by the end of the 1850s the British government had taken over direct control, and an Indian population of more than 250 million bowed to the imperial might of the British Raj. By the 1870s the holdings of the British Empire overseas were vast and growing. Africa and Asia had yet to be conquered, but the move to appoint Victoria empress of India marked a commitment to the permanence of British rule overseas.

Victoria was crowned queen of Great Britain and Ireland in 1837, at the age of eighteen. She ruled as queen of England for sixty-four years. The late Victorian period was a time of great expansion and colonization for the British Empire. It had military strength, economic power, and technological sophistication, and most countries were no match for the mighty British Empire. It was determined to bring the rest of the world under its control and very nearly did until well into World War I. Queen Victoria believed it was the duty of the British Empire to protect the poor natives and advance civilization. The belief that the English were entrusted by God to rule "lesser" nations is a quintessentially Victorian idea, but such beliefs are still somewhat prevalent even today. The English remained in India until as late as 1937.

David Gilmour is a visiting fellow at St. Anthony's College, Oxford. He is the author of *The Last Leopard: Guiseppe de Lampedusa* (1988) and, most recently, *Curzon* (1994). In the following essay, written for the *Wilson Quarterly*, Gilmour describes how Queen Victoria came to be appointed empress of India and tracks the progress of India under British rule and the significant ways in which the British have influenced Indian culture, law, and politics through the present day.

Until the last quarter of the 19th century, the ruler of the world's largest empire possessed no imperial title. Russia and Austria-Hungary had been ruled by emperors for centuries; Germany, recently united under Prussia, had just acquired its first, while France had just discarded its second. But Queen Victoria remained merely a queen until in 1876 her prime minister, Benjamin Disraeli, persuaded Parliament to make her empress of India.

The title was of purely symbolic significance: it did not apply to other parts of the empire and it did not even affect India, which continued to be administered by a viceroy responsible to the cabinet in London. But it reflected an increased sense of imperial purpose, a strong and growing belief in the permanence of British rule overseas. The empire still had a long way to expand: large territories in Africa and Asia had to be added before it could be claimed that a quarter of the globe was painted red. But 1876 may be seen as the apogee of imperial self-confidence. The 1857 Indian Mutiny, which briefly threatened British rule in the north, was almost a generation in the past; the "scramble for Africa" had not begun; and Britain's economic predominance was as yet unchallenged by Germany and the United States. Lord Mayo's belief that Britain should hold India "as long as the sun shines in heaven" was widely shared.

People with a Mission

The Victorian sense of empire was concentrated on India partly because of the subcontinent's strategic importance. As Lord Curzon, the queen's last viceroy, observed, the loss of India would reduce Britain to the status of a third-rate power. But India also provided the Victorians with an imperial calling which they could not pursue in other parts of the empire. Canada, Australia, and New

Zealand were settler societies responsible for their own govern-ment and without large native populations to administer. The South Africans had problems peculiar to themselves, but they too were white colonists with a hunger for land. When the writer John Buchan remarked that the empire was about "a sense of space in the blood," he was talking about the great and sparsely inhabited tracts of the white colonies. But in India, the Victorians were not colonists. They saw themselves as people with a mission, admin-istrators entrusted by Providence to rule India for the sake of the Indians and to implant British ideas of justice, law, and humanity.

It had not always been so. Since the 17th century, Britons had been sailing to India to enrich themselves. Many had been ad-venturers who risked the ravages of climate and disease to bring back large fortunes from Bengal. Some had liked India for itself, immersing themselves in native culture and adopting local styles of living. Both types became almost extinct in the Victorian period, victims alike of a high-minded and intolerant zeal for Westernization.

Victorian attitudes toward empire were shaped by the Evan-gelical and Utilitarian movements in Britain, neither of which had sympathy for Indian customs or religion. Many people dreamed fantastically of a mass conversion of Hindus to Chris-tianity. William Wilberforce, who was largely responsible for the abolition of the slave trade, regarded the conversion of India as even more important, "the greatest of all causes." And even though the number of converts from Hinduism turned out to be very small, the last Victorian bishop of Calcutta believed as late as 1915 that an Indian "Constantine" would emerge and bring his followers into the Christian fold.

Few of the administrators shared this aspiration. Curzon re-garded missionaries as a nuisance and believed that conversion was both improbable and undesirable. But members of the In-dian Civil Service (ICS), that elite body of 1,100 men that ad-ministered the Indian Empire, were heavily influenced by the idea of secular Westernization explicit in the writings of the Util-itarians. The crucial figure was the philosopher James Mill, who in 1806 began writing a six-volume history of British India, a study regarded by [English writer and politician] Thomas Babington Macaulay as "the greatest historical work" in English since [English historian] Edward Gibbon's *Decline and Fall of the Roman Empire.* Mill, who had never been to India and knew no Indian language, argued that Indian society was so barbarous and decadent that it could be redeemed only by a system of government and law based on Utilitarian principles. A number of British officials, such as Mountstuart Elphinstone, the governor of Bombay, were repelled by Mill's sarcasm, but they never refuted him in print. Mill's volumes became a textbook at Haileybury, the college established for entrants to the civil service, and were largely unchallenged for half a century.

The Real Villain

"Westernization" of course had its positive side: the practice of suttee or widow burning, was abolished, female infanticide was slowly reduced, and thugee—the ritual murder of travelers carried out by thugs devoted to the goddess Kali—was suppressed. India also benefited from judicial and administrative reforms as well as from the great surge of Victorian engineering, particularly the building of railways and canals for irrigation. But an inevitable result of Mill's thought was a deterioration in relations between British and Indians. Once it had been accepted that Indian society was barbarous and needed British help to reform itself, it was natural for the British to regard themselves as a superior race appointed to assist in the redemption of the barbarians. The consequent racial segregation—Indians in the bazaars and Britons in neat Civil Lines and army cantonments—is usually blamed on the racism and snobbery of Victorian ladies. But this is not fair. Many Victorian memsahibs no doubt were racist and snobbish, yet nobody has explained how they could have integrated into native society while Indian women, Hindus as well as Muslims, remained in purdah. The real villains were Mill's presumption and ignorance. Indian society was poorer and more backward than it had been in the 16th century, but solutions to its problems required both a sympathy and an understanding that a pseudohistorian in London simply did not possess.

Macaulay denigrated the East and extolled British virtues even more eloquently than Mill. His essays on Robert Clive and Warren Hastings, the two preeminent figures in the making of the 18th-century empire, encouraged the view that the acquisition of India had been an essentially heroic enterprise, a theater for the display of true British character. Just as [English privateer] Sir Francis Drake's plundering was played down in the making of the Elizabethan hero, so Clive's rapaciousness during his first Bengal governorship was brushed aside by the need to provide an exemplar of British virtues. Victorians were taught that their Indian Empire had been won against enormous odds by qualities familiar since the days of Agincourt: courage, self-sacrifice, duty, iron will. And if such qualities had been the formula for India's acquisition, it was logical to assume that these qualities could also be deployed for its retention. Sir James Stephen, a redoubtable administrator, defined English virtues as "the masterful will, the stout heart, the active brain, the calm nerves, the strong body."

Young district officers of the ICS were taught to believe that the future was in their hands. If they behaved as England expected, the Indians would accept them and the empire would be safe. So they dedicated their lives to the pursuit of justice, confident in their belief that all that these teeming districts needed was a solitary Englishman, straightforward and incorruptible, riding from village to village, setting up his table under a banyan tree and settling their disputes. It was an exhilarating experience, especially for young men fresh from Oxford University sent out to govern half a million people in areas the size of a large English county. What joy, one of them recalled, "feeling that one is working and ruling and making oneself useful in God's world."

Queen Victoria and her children

A Few Hundred Englishmen

Based though they may have been on bad history and false premises, Victorian beliefs contained much that was true. Clive may not have been a spotless hero, but his military and administrative records are remarkable. The ICS officers may have believed that they belonged to a superior race, but their administration was regarded by most Indians as just; villagers divided by religion, caste, and class were happy to accept judgments handed out by a pink-faced, unbribable young man who belonged to none of their subdivisions. The statistics demonstrate how broad that acceptance was and also indicate how Western views of Indian inferiority had permeated the Indians themselves. Even after the horrors of the 1857 mutiny, Britain kept only 65,000 white soldiers in an area populated by 300 million people that now includes not only India but Pakistan, Bangladesh, and Burma. In one district of Lower Bengal, 20 Britons lived among 2.5 million natives. As late as 1939, about 28 million Punjabis—people not renowned for their docility—were governed by 60 British civil servants. No wonders [Soviet leader Joseph] Stalin grumbled that it was absurd for India to be ruled by a few hundred Englishmen.

Nearly a century after the death of Queen Victoria, we can appreciate how precariously her Indian Empire rested on the self-confidence of its administrators. But this fragility was clear neither to most of them nor to foreign observers at the time. There seemed to be a solidity about the empire that enabled Theodore Roosevelt to compare its "admirable achievements" with those of the Romans. [Otto von] Bismarck, the German chancellor, once declared that "were the British Empire to disappear, its work in India would remain one of its lasting monuments," and even [Indian nationalist and spiritual leader Mohandas] Gandhi was inspired to say that "the British Empire existed for the welfare of the world." All of them could see that the government of India was a despotism, yet all believed that it was a stable and enlightened one. India helped to illustrate the boast that at home Britain was "Greek" while abroad it was "Roman."

Forever Bound Together

At the height of the Victorian empire, few people foresaw the day when India would no longer need Britain. The peoples of the two countries, believed Curzon, were tillers in the same field, jointly concerned with the harvest and ordained to walk along the same path for many years to come. Like others, he believed in the emergence of a new patriotism, common to both British and Indians, that would bind the two races forever. As he once told members of the Bengali Chamber of Commerce, "If I thought it were all for nothing, and that you or I were simply writing inscriptions on the sand to be washed out by the next tide, if I felt that we were not working here for the good of India in obedience to a higher law and a nobler aim, then I would see the link that holds England and India together severed without a sigh. But it is because I believe in the future of this country, and in the capacity of our race to guide it to goals that it has never hitherto attained, that I keep courage and press forward."

British imperialists had a special feeling for India, the oldest part of the empire, but the civilizing mission was directed also to Africa. Writing in the 1890s, the young Winston Churchill asked, "What enterprise is more noble and more profitable than the reclamation from barbarism of fertile regions and large populations? To give peace to warring tribes, to administer justice where all was violence, to strike the chains from the slave, to draw the richness from the soil, to plant the earliest seeds of commerce and learning, to increase in whole peoples their capacities for pleasure and diminish their chances of pain—what more beautiful ideal or more valuable reward can inspire human effort?"

Neither Curzon nor Churchill could envisage Britain without an empire. "We have to answer our helm," declared the former, "and it is an imperial helm, down all the tides of Time." Wherever peoples were living in backwardness or barbarism, "wherever ignorance or superstition is rampant, wherever enlightenment or progress [is] possible, wherever duty and self-sacrifice call—there is, as there has been for hundreds of years, the true summons of the Anglo-Saxon race." And if the race did not answer that summons, if Britain became a country with "no aspiration but a narrow and selfish materialism," it would end up merely "a sort of glorified Belgium."

Conflict of Interests

Although the empire continued to expand into the 1920s, the tide had begun to turn against the modern Rome at least a generation earlier. Toward the end of the 19th century, a growing number of ICS officers were beginning to feel that their duty should be not to preserve British India "as long as the sun shines in heaven" but to prepare the country for their eventual departure. Simultaneously, the Indian National Congress, founded in 1885 by a new breed of Indian nationalists, coupled protestations of loyalty and even gratitude to the empire with demands for greater Indian involvement in the administration. Like their sympathizers in the ICS, they understood the fundamental contradiction of the Victorian empire: that it was impossible to reconcile the imperial mission abroad with the liberal tradition at home. While in Africa the colonists were under no pressure to attempt that reconciliation, in India the issue was impossible to avoid. How, for example, could it be explained to [future Indian prime minister] Jawaharlal Nehru, who was educated at Harrow and Cambridge, that the British liberal tradition could be applied to him in England but not in India? How could it be argued that such a man was unfit to govern his own people?

Goaded by the Russian Revolution, the pressures of World War I, and the increasing talk of self-determination, the British government declared in 1917 that its goal—the same as Gandhi's later on—was self-rule for India within the British Empire. Much of course had to be resolved before self-rule became a reality, and an extra delay was caused by another world war. But, in 1947, the British finally let their liberalism triumph over their imperialism and withdrew peacefully from the subcontinent. The amicability of the withdrawal and the subsequent friendliness between the two peoples surprised observers such as Eleanor Roosevelt who were determined to see British India as a typical instance of colonial occupation. But there were few parallels with the situations in Algeria, Indochina, or anywhere else. Cheered by the populace, the last British regiment marched through Bombay's Gateway of India and sailed home. Despite differences over international issues, the respect and the affection remained: in 1979, when Lord Mountbatten was killed by an IRA bomb, the Indian Parliament went into recess to mourn the last British viceroy of their country. India's leaders still remembered that in 1947 the British had kept their promise and departed; they had not been ejected. At the time of independence, Rajendra Prasad, who became India's first president, sent a message to King George VI that helps explain Indian feelings toward their recent rulers: "While our achievement is in no small measure due to our sufferings and sacrifices, it is also the result of world forces and events; and last, but not least, it is the consummation and fulfillment of the historic traditions and democratic ideals of the British race."

The End of Empire

Within 20 years of its departure from India, Britain had withdrawn from nearly all the rest of its empire. Soon the great swathes of red paint were reduced to a handful of dots such as Hong Kong, Gibraltar, and the Falkland Islands. The center of the world's greatest empire was transformed into a modest European state. [American statesman] Dean Acheson famously observed that Britain had lost an empire and not found a role, but most Britons were in fact not looking for a role. They wanted to jettison the remaining parts of their empire as soon as possible and forget all about their imperial past. Politicians of the 1960s were concerned about joining the Common Market and making Britain a more civilized society by measures such as decriminalizing homosexuality and abolishing capital punishment. Historians sought to write India out of their island story or, where this was not possible, to disparage the achievements of the ICS and overestimate the importance of the Indian National Congress. Clive was reduced from the status of schoolboy hero to that of a worthy soldier who owed his success to the wealth of Bengal and the strength of the British navy.

Exhilarated by the radical spirit and hedonism of the 1960s, people in Britain looked back at the empire with a mixture of guilt and embarrassment. The change in national status was so overwhelming that it could be managed only by rejecting or belittling the past. Even the adjective Victorian, referring as it does to the greatest period of national consequence, became a term of mockery and abuse, aimed at the reactionary, the prudish, and the old-fashioned. Britons congratulated themselves on having shed every remnant of that age. They visited India for its gurus and its mysticism, not because their grandparents had lived there or because the subcontinent was so bound up with their history that it contained two million British graves. All they needed from the imperial past was [English novelist] E.M. Forster's *Passage to India*—and later the film David Lean made of it—to convince them that the Raj was both stupid and morally wrong. They were much comforted too by Richard Attenborough's film *Gandhi*, which pandered to anti-Raj feeling, not least by having Lord Irwin, the benign young viceroy who was trusted and admired by Gandhi, played by Sir John Gielgud in his late seventies as a cantankerous martinet always itching to throw Gandhi in jail.

Victorian Values

In the 1980s, the emergence of a tepid Raj nostalgia (illustrated by the growth of Indian restaurants in Britain with names such as "Lancers" and "The Indian Cavalry Club") coincided with [Prime Minister] Margaret Thatcher's call for a return to "Victorian values" at home. Unfortunately, this term was exploited by both the prime minister and her critics for purposes of propaganda. To Thatcher, "Victorian values" primarily meant enterprise and self-reliance, while her left-wing critics talked about Victorian hypocrisy and reminded the nation of child chimney sweeps and Dickensian slums. Both sides regarded "Victorian values" as part of a remote past; neither saw nor attempted to see how many of the true Victorian values had survived in Britain and even abroad. Most of the ideals of [Prime Minister] William Gladstone, who symbolizes the Victorian age much better than its queen, are still among the ideals of British parliamentarians: liberty, free trade, international cooperation, representative government, and a foreign policy based on moral considerations as well as national interest. British political leaders often fail lamentably to uphold them, but they remain the ideals. Britons may have consigned the empire to remote and inaccurate history, but many of its values are still with them.

Ironically, the Victorian empire is remembered more clearly in India than in Britain. Indeed, the Indian people are more aware of the whole Indo-British connection than the British are. Although some of them might like to expunge the Raj from their past, too much of its legacy remains in their institutions and on their ground. The British can distance themselves from their imperial past in a way which the Indians are denied. Arriving in the colorful anarchy of modern India, visitors might feel initially that the country has cut all links with the colonial epoch. But awareness of how much of the connection still survives will soon follow, not just among the great Victorian buildings of Bombay or in the imperial capital of New Delhi but among the people and their institutions. The civil service and the judiciary system are both descendants of the Victorian era, while parliamentary government is a legacy of later British rule. Democracy is far from perfect in India as elsewhere, but it is infinitely preferable to the regimes offered by its neighbors, China and Pakistan, over the last 50 years. And at a cultural level, English is now more widely spoken in India than ever and remains the only means of communication between an educated Hindi speaker in the north and an educated Tamil from the south.

A Surprising Legacy

But the most vibrant Victorian legacy, one that would have astonished the Victorians themselves, is the game of cricket. This sedate sport, designed for English afternoons on village greens and school playing fields, remains almost incomprehensible outside the boundaries of the former British Empire. Yet in India, as in Pakistan, Sri Lanka, and the West Indies, it is played with a kind of baseball vigor and enthusiasm quite alien to England. The visitor to an Indian city on a Sunday will witness an extraordinary sight: crowded into every square yard of parks, gardens, alleys, and even cemeteries, thousands of Indian boys will be playing cricket, hitting and running and all the time shouting in antiquated English jargon. In India, cricket is truly what it never became in England—the national sport.

The Making of a Dictator

by Henry Bamford Parkes

Porfirio Díaz came into office promising many democratic reforms but ended up ruling Mexico for thirty-four years as an absolute dictator. His initial plan, known as the Plan of Tuxtepec, was designed to develop and protect constitutional democracy and to stimulate economic development. He abandoned his goals but did make many important economic reforms and opened the country to foreign investment. In the process of modernization, however, the human toll was high, class distinctions were polarized, and Mexico was changed forever.

Born in Oaxaca, Mexico, in 1830, Díaz was a mestizo (part Indian) and of humble origin. He began training for the Catholic priesthood but left the seminary and joined the army when war broke out with the United States in 1846. Díaz became a military leader and served until 1867, when Maximilian became emperor after the French-Mexican war. Díaz resigned his command in the military and returned to Oaxaca, but he continued to lead political protests and military revolts against foreign rule. In November 1876 Díaz defeated the government forces of President Sebastián Lerdo de Tejada, and in May 1877 he was formally elected president of Mexico.

Henry Bamford Parkes is an author and historian who has published many articles and books, including *The American Experience: An Interpretation of the History and Civilization of the American People* and *Jonathan Edwards: The Fiery Puritan*. The following essay is from his book *A History of Mexico*. It describes

Porfirio Díaz's ascent to power and how he became such a powerful and lasting political figure.

The alleged intention of the Plan of Tuxtepec [Díaz's plan for democracy] had been to protect constitutional government; intellectuals of the calibre of Ignacio Ramírez and Riva Palacio had supported it, in the belief that Díaz was the embodiment of Mexican democracy. Yet its result was to give Mexico a master more powerful than any she had ever known before. Porfirio Díaz was to govern the country—save for one four-year interlude—for the next thirty-four years and to transform the constitution into a personal dictatorship.

Peace Must Be Enforced

The Reform had had two purposes: to establish a democratic form of government; and to stimulate economic development. Under [former president Benito] Juárez these purposes had been combined; under Díaz the first was sacrificed for the sake of the second. According to the apologists of the Díaz régime democracy was impossible in Mexico; it meant, in practice, anarchy and the domination of the provincial *caciques* [local chiefs]. Díaz set himself to enforce peace by making himself the national *cacique*, binding together the various discordant elements in the Mexican population through a common bond of loyalty to himself. Only a dictator, it was argued, could enforce peace, while without peace Mexico's natural resources could not be developed, and without economic development education and social reform and the protection of national sovereignty from the encroachments of the United States were impossible.

Díaz could easily persuade himself that Mexico needed a master. Even Juárez had been compelled to interfere with elections. But Díaz had little of the enlightenment which had characterized the leaders of the Reform. A Mixtec Indian with a little Spanish blood, half educated—to the end of his life he could not write Spanish correctly—and with the crude manners of a guerrilla chieftain, he had now allowed himself to be dominated by greed for power. He was loyal, even when his control of Mexico was absolute, to a certain sense of morality. Though he killed his enemies, he did not kill wantonly or unnecessarily; and considering his opportunities, he showed a remarkable degree of financial integrity. But though he was neither a murderer nor a thief, he tolerated such crimes in others, and he was responsible for blunders which were worse than crimes. With all his extraordinary subtlety in the handling of men, Díaz retained to the end of his life the simple and unsophisticated outlook of an Indian warrior. He was too insensitive to realize that the suppression of political freedom and the enslavement of the masses might be too high a price to pay for material prosperity, and too ignorant to understand the economic forces which, during his régime, were sweeping across Mexico. Díaz himself, like a power of nature, can scarcely be judged in moral terms; but the nation which has not learned how to control such men pays a heavy penalty.

An Attack on the Sheepfolds

The guiding principle of the Díaz dictatorship was expressed in the phrase *pan ó palo*, bread or the club. To all dangerous elements, even to men whom he knew to be his personal enemies, Díaz offered power, prestige, and the opportunity of enriching themselves; as Díaz himself cynically remarked, a dog with a bone in its mouth neither kills nor steals. If they refused the offer, then he crushed them mercilessly. He stimulated rivalries and quarrels between the different groups whom he had attached to his government, so that they would never unite in a palace conspiracy or a coup d état, while at the same time he maintained his own popularity with the Mexican people by allowing his subordinates to take the blame for tyranny and injustice. Such a program necessarily meant a cessation of social reform. Juárez had wished to lead Mexico towards democracy; Díaz proposed merely to enforce peace. In Díaz's 'policy of conciliation' what was considered was not the permanent well-being of the Mexican nation but how far any particular faction might become dangerous to the dictatorship. The various groups who for the past half-century had been instigating plans and *pronunciamentos* [military coups]—the landowners, the clergy, the generals, the *caciques*, the foreign-born capitalists, the office-hunting middle classes, the intelligentsia, even the brigand chieftains—all these were converted into faithful adherents of Don Porfirio. The people who were ignored in the distribution of favors were the peasant and proletarian masses who—without leadership—had no means of asserting their interests. The meaning of the Porfirian dictatorship was that the bands of wolves, instead of fighting each other as they had been doing ever since the establishment of independence, were now invited to join each other in an attack on the sheepfolds. Peace achieved by such methods could scarcely be permanent; and when senile decay brought about the fall of the dictator, the accumulated resentment of the masses burst out into social revolution.

Whether a more enlightened and less cynical statesmanship could have given Mexico peace is questionable. Díaz had found a formula for ending civil war, and for the first time since the establishment of the Republic Mexico was able to devote herself to economic development. It was in the methods by which he stimulated that development, rather than in his political program, that Díaz committed his most disastrous blunders. Wishing to encourage the investment of money from abroad, he gave away Mexico's national resources to foreign entrepreneurs. Proposing to transform Mexico into a capitalistic nation, he allowed the Indians to be robbed of such lands as they still possessed. Industrialization was imposed mercilessly and recklessly, without plan or forethought, and with no attempt to mitigate its evils, upon a country which was not ready for it. The national income and the revenues of the government enormously increased; but Díaz's successors had to undertake the complex and delicate task of undoing much of what Díaz had done. They had to regain national ownership of the wealth which Díaz had lavished upon foreigners; and they had to change the Indians from peons back again into independent peasants.

Reuniting a Shattered Party

Díaz knew how to be patient, and during his first term he was careful not to alienate his supporters by any sudden usurpation of power. Distributing his favors impartially among *Juaristas* [supporters of former president Juárez], *Lerdistas* [supporters of former president Lerdo de Tejada], and *Porfiristas*, he reunited, under his own leadership, the various factions of the shattered liberal party. The army generals and the provincial *caciques* were neutralized by the device of playing them off against each other; ambitious generals were given commands in areas where they would quarrel with state governors, and discontented governors were placed under the surveillance of generals whom Díaz could trust. The press and judiciary remained relatively free, and only one incident caused any serious outcry against executive authority.

When, in 1879, there was a Lerdist conspiracy at Vera Cruz, Díaz telegraphed to the governor, Mier y Terán, that the conspirators should be executed immediately. Mier y Terán promptly shot nine persons who had, apparently, no connection with the conspiracy.

By the end of his term Díaz was able to dictate his successor. After stimulating rivalries among his leading subordinates by encouraging each of them to hope for the succession, he threw the prize to Manuel González. González was a soldier, who had fought by his side against the French and in the revolution of Tuxtepec; Díaz respected soldiers, whereas he despised civilian politicians. González, moreover, was his friend, whom he could trust to restore the presidency in 1884; and he guessed, perhaps, that even if González himself were tempted by thoughts of re-election, there would be no danger that the Mexican people, after being governed by him for four years, would give him any encouragement.

Partnership with the Church

Díaz's second term elevated a new adherent to the leading position in the cabinet and marked a new development in the 'policy of conciliation.' Romero Rubio, formerly Lerdo's political manager, had gone into exile in 1876, but had rapidly realized that he had backed the wrong candidate. He had returned to Mexico and attached himself to Díaz, putting at Díaz's disposal his remarkable talents for political intrigue. Lerdo, he explained, had gone mad, and he was afraid that the disease might be catching. In 1881 Díaz, already fifty-one years of age, was married to Romero Rubio's young daughter, Carmen, or Carmelita. Romero Rubio became Díaz's secretary of *gobernación* [corresponding roughly to the U.S. secretary of the interior, but relatively more important]; he managed congress and controlled the police, while his ownership of the illegal gambling houses in the capital enabled him to finance a corps of *bravi* [gangsters], who could be used to intimidate such political opponents as were beyond the reach of judicial procedure. . . . Carmelita had been educated as a Catholic, and after her marriage her spiritual advisor arranged a meeting between Díaz and Archbishop Labastida. It was secretly agreed that clerical appointments should be submitted to Díaz for his approval, and, in return, that the Laws of Reform should not be enforced. Monasteries and nunneries were again established, and—through a series of legal fictions—the Church again began to accumulate property. It was a bargain by which Díaz was the chief beneficiary. The clergy gratefully used their influence to preach obedience to the dictator, knowing that the laws remained on the statute book and that Díaz could enforce them if he pleased. When, early in the twentieth century, a small section of the Mexican clergy began to advocate social reform, the Catholic hierarchy saw to it that the Church should do nothing which might antagonize the government. Thus the clergy sacrificed their opportunity of identifying themselves with the cause of the people and became again, as under the Spanish kings, the instruments of a despotism. For the Mexican Church this bargain was to be ruinous.

Loyalty Is Lucrative

During his second term Díaz so tightened his control over the country that opposition became impossible. An object-lesson for rivals was provided by García de la Cadena, a general who was rumored to be plotting rebellion and who was accordingly murdered by local officials in Zacatecas. Sudden death in one shape or another was the fate of other ambitious chieftains. [General] Corona, one of the heroes of the war with the French, was assassinated by a lunatic. There was no evidence implicating Díaz, but it began to be said that presidential ambition was a disease which usually ended fatally. To any of his associates who seemed anxious for the succession, even to his own father-in-law, Díaz would drop hints about the untimely death of García de la Cadena. Loyalty to the government was lucrative; the number of salaried positions and commercial monopolies at Díaz's disposal was steadily increasing. Opposition, on the other hand, even when not fatal, was usually costly; Díaz knew how to adjust the tax assessment schedules so that his enemies would pay heavily.

The state governors became instruments of the dictatorship. The device of playing them off against the army generals was still effective. . . . Thus all the state governors became Díaz appointees; many of them were re-elected almost as often as the dictator himself, while others could transmit the succession to their relatives. As a reward for loyalty they were allowed to tyrannize over their dependents, murdering political opponents and becoming owners of *haciendas* and liquor monopolies and illegal gambling houses. Thus the Reform, instead of destroying the old feudalism, had ended in the creation of a new one; alongside the old creole *hacendados* [landowners] had developed a new *mestizo* nobility of ex-liberal chieftains. . . . By contrast with most of the local officials Díaz was a model of honesty and humanity. Nobody would wish to overthrow Díaz in order to give the presidency to one of his state governors.

Elections Are a Formality

With the state administrations controlled by Díaz, elections became a mere formality, and congress consisted of Díaz's nominees. Díaz would compile a list of those persons whom he wished to reward with seats in congress, and the list was distributed among the local officials. He would include anybody who had happened to win his favor—giving a seat, for example, to a dentist whom he had called in suddenly to attend to an aching tooth—with a special preference for natives of his own state of Oaxaca. Any congressman who displeased the dictator would be omitted from the list at the next election. Occasionally mistakes occurred, and the names were included of persons who were already dead; but in general the forms of the franchise were scrupulously observed. Voting, however, soon tended to disappear, since the victorious candidates were known before the election. In one state, in order to preserve an appearance of electoral enthusiasm, the task of filling out a sufficient number of ballot papers was entrusted to prisoners in the state penitentiary.

According to the constitution the subordinate magistrates were appointed by the supreme court, while the court itself was elected in the same manner as the president. Such an arrangement made it easy for Díaz to dominate the judiciary. The general rule which Díaz imposed was that foreigners, especially Americans, should always receive favorable verdicts, while Mexicans of wealth and position could win lawsuits as long as they had the dictator's approval. For the peasants and the proletariat justice did not exist. The army was recruited by forced levies, and any of the lower orders who were so unfortunate as to offend members of the reigning bureaucracy were quickly drafted into service. Criminals—under which description were included any who resisted the tyranny of local *jefes políticos* [political bosses] or the greed of local landowners—were transported to Quintana Roo or to the Valle Nacional in Oaxaca, where they were sold as laborers to the plantation owners and where—working in chain gangs from dawn until sunset under a tropical sun—they usually died within a year. Rural Mexico was pacified by the simple device of transforming the bandits into policemen. Díaz's celebrated *rurales*, wearing broad felt hats, grey uniforms with red ties and silver buttons, and silver-embossed saddles, made Mexico one of the safest countries in the world—for all except Mexicans. For the first time in the history of Mexico banditry almost disappeared, but the ex-bandits who now wore government uniforms could still exercise their old professional proclivities at the expense of the peasants. . . . They were allowed to shoot their prisoners, explaining afterwards that the prisoners had been killed while attempting to escape. There were more than ten thousand cases of *ley fuga* during the Díaz régime.

Opposition Proved Fatal

The rule of bread or the club enabled Díaz to win the support of the intelligentsia. The bureaucracy was constantly expanding; between 1876 and 1910 the government payroll increased by nine hundred per cent; and the Mexican middle class were only too willing to serve the dictator in return for substantial and regularly paid salaries. No intellectual was independent of the government. Education, apart from a few Catholic schools and seminaries, was state-controlled. The press was subsidized, even the opposition press, which was used by Díaz to undermine cabinet officials who were becoming too popular. A few editors were bold enough to attack the dictator himself, but they did so in the expectation of prison sentences. The right of jury trials for press offences, established by the constitution, had been abolished by González. Henceforth journalists could be convicted of libel or sedition by the decision of a single magistrate. Outside the federal district nobody's life was safe, and half a dozen journalists were murdered by state governors. Díaz tolerated mild criticisms, but sent journalists to the typhus-infested prison of Belem or the water-logged dungeons of San Juan de Uloa whenever they became dangerous. Filomeno Mata, who had supported the revolution of Tuxtepec, went to prison thirty-four times. The result was that there was no serious intellectual opposition to the dictatorship; consequently no intellectual preparation for the revolution which followed its collapse. . . .

The Economy Flourishes

[Díaz's] primary preoccupation was the budget; however efficient his political methods might be, only a treasury surplus could guarantee the stability of the dictatorship. During the eighties and nineties capital was pouring into Mexico from Europe and the United States, and every branch of economic activity was making astonishing progress. Before the end of the century more than nine thousand miles of railroads had been built. The output of the mines, stimulated by the new cyanide process applied to precious metals and increased by the opening of lead and copper mines, rose from a value of about thirty million pesos in 1880 to more than ninety millions in 1900. New plantations were producing sugar, coffee, henequen, cotton, rubber, and tropical fruits; textile mills in Vera Cruz, iron and steel works in Nuevo León had initiated Mexico's industrial revolution. The annual value of Mexican foreign trade, which had amounted to fifty million pesos in the seventies, exceeded two hundred millions by the end of the century. Revenue steadily increased, but through the eighties expenditure more than kept pace with it. The recognition of the English debt enabled Díaz to borrow abroad, but interest and discount rates were still excessive. In 1892, as a result of a bad harvest and of the depreciation of silver in the world market, the treasury was again in difficulties. This year was the crucial one of the Díaz dictatorship, for it was marked also by a revival of political opposition. In 1888 Díaz had re-elected himself without formality, but in 1892 there were demonstrations demanding a free election. Díaz decided to make a gesture towards democracy. A new party, the Liberal Union, was organized; and though the party convention performed its function of nominating Díaz for re-election, its leaders were allowed to criticize the dictatorship. . . . The liberals were persuaded to support Díaz as the only alternative to anarchy, but they were encouraged to believe that the dictatorship was only transitional and that a free press and a free judiciary would soon be conceded. Meanwhile irreconcilable enemies of the dictatorship went to prison in the City of Mexico and suffered *ley fuga* in the provinces.

Re-election safely achieved, Díaz forgot about the free press and the free judiciary and resumed his battle with the financial crisis. In 1893 the treasury was transferred to a young man who was to dominate the later years of the dictatorship, José Ives Limantour. It was Limantour who reaped the fruits of the long struggle. . . . In 1894, with expenditure at forty-one millions and revenue at forty-three millions, Mexico, for the first time in her history as an independent nation, achieved a balanced budget.

The corner once turned, there was no looking back. By the year 1910 the revenues of the federal government had reached one hundred and ten millions, and those of the states and the municipalities, eleven millions in the time of Juárez, had risen to sixty-four millions. The total surplus during the last sixteen years of the dictatorship was one hundred and thirty-six millions, more than half of which remained as a cash reserve in the treasury. Henceforth Díaz and his supporters could flatter themselves that peace was assured. They could now easily buy off all opposition, and if more money were needed, the credit of the government was good and loans could be made on easy terms abroad. Every Mexican revolution—it was argued—had been the work of unpaid generals and bureaucrats; deficits had led to *pronunciamentos*, and *pronunciamentos* had led, in turn, to more deficits. But the political genius and the iron will of Don Porfirio had broken the vicious circle and made revolution impossible. The dictator, now sixty-four years old, settled down to enjoy the blaze of glory which was to surround him for the next sixteen years.

An Army Surgeon's Account of the Battle of Isandlwana

by James Henry Reynolds

Great Britain's annexation of the Zulu territory in southern Africa proved to be a tragic and difficult campaign. British soldiers marched into Zululand expecting the Zulus to quickly lay down their arms. Instead, the British were confronted with a fierce, organized, and disciplined Zulu army. When the Zulus met the invading British forces with their spears at the Battle of Isandlwana, they engaged and defeated the pride of the British colonial army, a feat that has gone down in history as one of the most glorious and spectacular achievements in world struggles to resist foreign domination. For the first time in history, the might of the colonial British forces was seriously challenged by native forces. Faced with the might of the superior army, the heroic Zulu warriors knew no fear. They shed rivers of blood to remain free in the land that was undoubtedly theirs.

While the invading British column at Isandlwana was being wiped out by a forty-thousand-strong Zulu force, another group of four thousand Zulu warriors made its way over the hill to Rorke's

James Henry Reynolds, "Surgeon Reynolds' Account of the Battle," *Journal of the Royal Army Medical Corps*, 1928.

Drift. There, a British missionary station and a makeshift army hospital came under attack. A garrison of about eighty British soldiers defended thirty sick and wounded soldiers and a handful of hospital personnel and medical staff. Close combat lasted for more than twelve hours, but the besieged men were able to keep their attackers at bay. By dawn, the remaining exhausted Zulus finally departed. But this would not be the last of the attacks, and the British would not always fare well.

The scramble for the African territories was long, costly, and involved aggressive warfare with natives as well as other European nations vying for the same resources. The British, in particular, conducted their campaign rapaciously, haphazardly, and without any long-term strategy. Ironically, in the end, the African colonies afforded the British and other European countries little economic gain except for a small area in the south. Many of the valuable resources in Africa could be found elsewhere at lesser expense, and the British people had little interest in African goods and handicrafts. In a war that was deliberately provoked by the British, the Zulu army gave a clear motive that a time comes in the life of people when there is only one way out—the way of challenging oppression by force and violence.

James Henry Reynolds was a staff surgeon stationed at the small army hospital that was the object of attack by the Zulus in the early morning of January 23, 1879. He made the following journal entry into the log of the Royal Army Medical Corps immediately after the Zulu attack at Rorke's Drift. The entry describes the attack and how the Royal Army Hospital Corps defended itself.

At 1:30 a large body of natives marched over the slope of Isandhlwana in our direction, their purpose evidently being to examine ravines and ruined kraals for hiding fugitives. These men we took to be our native contingent. Soon afterwards appeared four horsemen on the Natal side of the river galloping in the direction of our post, one of them was a regular soldier, and feeling they might possibly be messengers for additional medical assistance, I hurried down to the hospital as they rode up. They looked awfully scared, and I was at once startled to find one of them was riding Surgeon-Major Shepherd's pony. They shouted frantically, "The camp at Isandhlwana has been taken by the enemy and all our men in it massacred, that no power could stand against the enormous number of the Zulus, and the only chance for us all was in immediate flight." Lieutenant Bromhead, Acting-Commissary Dalton, and myself, forthwith consulted together, Lieutenant Chard not having as yet joined us from the pontoon, and we quickly decided that with barricades well placed around our present position a stand could best be made where we were. Just at this period Mr. Dalton's energies were invaluable. Without the smallest delay, he called upon his men to carry the mealie sacks here and there for defenses. Lieutenant Chard (R.E.) arrived as this work was in progress, and gave many useful orders as regards the lines of defense. He approved also of the hospital being taken in, and between the hospital orderlies, convalescent patients (eight or ten) and myself, we loopholed the building and made a continuation of the commissariat defences round it. The hospital however, occupied a wretched position, having a garden and shrubbery close by, which afterwards proved so favourable to the enemy; but comparing our prospects with that of the Isandhlwana affair, we felt that the mealie barriers might afford us a moderately fair chance.

At about 3:30 the enemy made their first appearance in a large crowd on the hospital side of our post, coming on in skirmishing order at a slow slinging run. We opened fire on them from the hospital at 600 yards, and although the bullets ploughed through their midst and knocked over many, there was no check or alteration made in their approach. As they got nearer they became more scattered, but the bulk of them rushed for the hospital and the garden in front of it.

The Zulus Pressed Forward

We found ourselves quickly surrounded by the enemy with their strong force holding the garden and shrubbery. From all sides but especially the latter places, they poured on us a continuous fire, to which our men replied as quickly as they could reload their rifles. Again and again the Zulus pressed forward and retreated, until at last they forced themselves so daringly, and in such numbers, as to climb over the mealie sacks in front of the hospital, and drove the defenders from there behind an entrenchment of biscuit boxes, hastily formed with much judgement and forethought by Lieutenant Chard. A heavy fire from behind it was resumed with renewed confidence, and with little confusion or delay, checking successfully the natives, and permitting a semi flank fire from another part of the laager to play on them destructively. At this time too, the loopholes in the hospital were made great use of. It was however, only temporary, as, after a short respite, they came on again with renewed vigour. Some of them gained the hospital verandah, and there got hand to hand with our men defending the doors. Once they were driven back from here, but other soon pressed forward in their stead, and having occupied the verandah in larger numbers than before, pushed their way right into the hospital, where confusion on our side naturally followed. Everyone tried to escape as best they could, and owing to the rooms not communicating with one another, the difficulties were insurmountable. Private Hook, 2/24th Regiment, who was acting as hospital cook, and Private Connolly, 2/24th Regiment, a patient in hospital, made their way into the open at the back of the hospital by breaking a hole in the wall. Most of the patients escaped through a small window looking into what may be styled the neutral ground. Those who madly tried to get off by leaving the front of the hospital were all killed with the exception of Gunner Howard.

An All-Night Attack

The only men actually killed in the hospital were three, excluding a Kaffir under treatment for compound fracture of the femur. The names were Sergeant Maxfield, Private Jenkins, both unable to assist in their escape, being debilitated by fever, and Private Adams, who was well able to move about, but could not be persuaded to leave his temporary refuge in a small room. The engagement continued more or less until about 7 o'clock P.M. and then, when we were beginning to consider our situation as rather hopeless, the fire from our opponents appreciably slackened giving us some time for reflection. Lieutenant Chard here again shined in resource. Anticipating the Zulus making one more united dash for the fort, and possibly gaining entrance, he converted an immense stack of mealies standing in the middle of our enclosure, and originally cone fashioned, into a comparatively safe place for a last retreat. Just as it was completed, smoke from the hospital appeared and shortly burst into flames. During the whole night following desultory fire was carried on by the enemy, and several feigned attacks were made, but nothing of a continued or determined effort was again attempted by them.

About 6 o'clock A.M., we found, after careful reconnoitring, that all the Zulus with the exception of a couple of stragglers had left our immediate vicinity, and soon afterwards a large body of men were seen at a distance marching towards us.

I do not think it possible that men could have behaved better than did the 2/24th and the Army Hospital Corps (three), who were particularly forward during the whole attack.

1860
The kingdom of Italy is established.

1860–1872
The second Maori War between British colonists and native New Zealanders takes place on the North Island. At the end of the largely guerrilla war, the natives were granted half the island.

1861
Emancipation of the Russian Serfs is proclaimed by Czar Alexander II, the central event of the Great Reform Era in Russian history (1856–1863); Louis Pasteur invents pasteurization to preserve milk, beer, and other foods; Abraham Lincoln is inaugurated as sixteenth president of the United States.

1861–1865
The American Civil War begins on April 12, 1861; eleven southern states secede from the United States.

1862
Lincoln issues the Emancipation Proclamation, which declares all slaves free; Otto von Bismarck becomes Prussian prime minister; Victor Hugo publishes *Les Misérables;* French occupation of Indochina (South Vietnam) begins.

1863
French troops occupy Mexico City and install Maximilian as emperor; Lincoln delivers the Gettysburg Address.

1864
Italy renounces its claim to Rome; Florence is made the capital in place of Turin; Karl Marx helps establish the First International Working Men's Association to promote socialism; the In-

ternational Red Cross is founded in Geneva, Switzerland; Leo Tolstoy publishes *War and Peace.*

1865
General Robert E. Lee surrenders to Union general Ulysses S. Grant on April 9 at Appomattox Court House to end the American Civil War; first transatlantic cable is laid, dramatically increasing speed of global communications; Thirteenth Amendment to the U.S. Constitution abolishes slavery; President Lincoln is assassinated April 14; Lewis Carroll publishes *Alice in Wonderland.*

1866
Prussian-Italian alliance against Austria is formed; Prussia invades Saxony, Hanover, and Hesse and takes lead in the process of German unification; Treaty of Vienna ends Austro-Italian war; Alfred Nobel invents dynamite.

1867
Napoléon III withdraws troops from Mexico; Maximilian is executed; Austro-Hungarian dual monarchy is formed; United States purchases Alaska from Russia for $7.2 million; Karl Marx publishes the first volume of *Das Kapital.*

1868
During the revolution in Spain, Queen Isabel II is deposed and flees to France; Meiji reform in Japan, shogunate abolished, and Japanese society is modernized; Louisa May Alcott publishes *Little Women.*

1869
Suez Canal opens to international shipping; John Stuart Mill publishes *On the Subjection of Women;* Dmitry Ivanovich Mendeleyev devises a periodic table for the classification of chemical elements; Pope Pius IX declares papal infallibility at meeting of First Vatican Council; authority in all matters of faith and morals to lie with the pope.

1870
The Franco-Prussian War begins; France declares war on Prussia and is defeated at Weissenberg; siege of Paris by Prussian

troops; French troops withdraw from Rome, which becomes Italy's capital.

1871
King of Prussia, William I, is elected German emperor at Versailles; the Commune in Paris rules the city for two months as first proletariat government; France capitulates; cedes Alsace-Lorraine to Germany; British Parliament legalizes labor unions; Charles Darwin publishes *The Descent of Man*, applying evolution by natural selection to humans.

1872
Civil war in Spain begins; Don Carlos escapes to France; Three-Emperors League is established in Berlin; alliance is formed between Germany, Russia, and Austria-Hungary; Eadweard Muybridge photographs a horse in motion as an early moving picture.

1873
Financial panic in Vienna and New York ushers in a global economic depression that lasts most of the 1870s; German troops evacuate France; massive famine in Madras and western India kills several million people; Ashtanti tribes fight British colonial troops in West Africa.

1874
Benjamin Disraeli becomes British prime minister; Britain annexes Fiji Islands; first impressionist exhibition held in Paris.

1875
The German Social Democratic Party, first mass Socialist Party in Europe, is established; Kwang Hsu becomes emperor of China; Richard M. Hoe of New York invents rotary printing press; Britain buys 176,602 Suez shares from Khedive of Egypt.

1876
The International Association for the Exploration and Civilization of Africa is established under the sponsorship of Belgian king Leopold II; Alexander Graham Bell invents the telephone; Lieutenant Colonel George Armstrong Custer and the entire seventh cavalry are killed at the Battle of the Little Bighorn; Serbia and Montenegro declare war on Turkey.

1877

Queen Victoria is proclaimed empress of India, symbolizing the triumph of British rule over the subcontinent; the Satsuma Rebellion, the final revolt of the samurai in Japan, is suppressed by the modern Meiji army; Louis Pasteur introduces his germ theory of disease, leading to the development of vaccines and the discovery of viruses; Russia declares war on Turkey and invades Rumania; Russians cross Danube and storm Kars; Russians take Plevna, Bulgaria; Bismarck declines to intervene; Thomas Alva Edison invents the phonograph; Porfirio Díaz is elected president of Mexico and rules as absolute dictator for thirty-four years.

1878

Greece declares war on Turkey; treaties of San Stefano and Berlin reshape the Balkans; Serbia, Rumania, and Montenegro gain independence; David Hughes invents the microphone; anti-Socialist law is enacted in Germany.

1879

The British-Zulu war occurs; Zulus massacre British soldiers in Isandlwana; British capture Cetewayo; Zulus eventually defeated and sign peace treaty with British; British invade Afghanistan at Kabul to counter Russian expansion; Britain and France resume joint control of the Suez Canal and Egypt's finances; Swedish dramatist Henrik Ibsen's *A Doll's House* premieres; German physicist Albert Einstein (1921 Nobel Prize) is born; Thomas Edison invents the lightbulb; the first electric streetcars are introduced in Germany.

FOR FURTHER RESEARCH

Stephen E. Ambrose, *Crazy Horse and Custer: The Parallel Lives of Two American Warriors.* Illus. Kenneth Francis Dewey. Garden City, NY: Doubleday, 1975.

————, *Nothing Like It in the World: The Men Who Built the Transcontinental Railroad, 1863–1869.* New York: Simon & Schuster, 2000.

Herbert Asbury, *Gangs of New York.* New York: A.A. Knopf, 1928.

Isaac Asimov, *Asimov's Chronicle of the World.* New York: HarperCollins, 1991.

C.A. Bayly, *Indian Society and the Making of the British Empire.* New York: Cambridge University Press, 1988.

Isaiah Berlin, *Karl Marx: His Life and Environment.* New York: Oxford University Press, 1996.

Gail Lee Bernstein, ed., *Recreating Japanese Women, 1600–1945.* Berkeley: University of California Press, 1980.

Otto von Bismarck, *Reflections and Reminiscences.* Trans. A.J. Butler. 2 vols. New York: Howard Fertig, 1966.

Jerome Blum, *Lord and Peasant in Russia.* Princeton, NJ: Princeton University Press, 1971.

Chris M. Calkins, *The Appomattox Campaign, March 29–April 9, 1865.* Conshohocken, PA: Combined Books, 1997.

Terrell Carver, ed., *Marx: Later Political Writings.* Cambridge, New York: Cambridge University Press, 1996.

G.D.H. Cole, *Socialist Thought: Marxism and Anarchism, 1850–1890.* New York: St. Martin's, 1964.

Benedetto Croce, *A History of Italy, 1871–1915.* Trans. Cecilia M. Ady. New York: Russell & Russell, 1963.

Charles Darwin, *The Autobiography of Charles Darwin, 1809–1882*. Ed. Nora Barlow. New York: Norton, 1993.

Stewart Edwards, *The Paris Commune, 1871*. London: Eyre and Spottiswoode, 1971.

Terence Emmons, *Emancipation of the Russian Serfs*. New York: Holt, Rinehart, and Winston, 1970.

Robert Ferguson, *Henrik Ibsen: A New Biography*. London: Richard Cohen Books, 1996.

D.K. Fieldhouse, *Colonialism, 1870–1945: An Introduction*. London: Weidenfeld and Nicolson, 1981.

Eric Foner, *Nothing but Freedom: Emancipation and Its Legacy*. Baton Rouge: Louisiana State University Press, 1983.

Andre Gunder Frank, *Capitalism and Underdevelopment in Latin America*. New York: Monthly Review Press, 1967.

Paul Garner, *Porfirio Díaz*. New York: Longman, 2001.

David Gillard, *The Struggle for Asia, 1828–1914: A Study in British and Russian Imperialism*. London: Methuen, 1977.

Bernard Grun, *The Timetables of History*. New York: Simon & Schuster, 1991.

Jeff Guy, *The Destruction of the Zulu Kingdom: The Civil War in Zululand, 1879–1884*. London: Longman, 1979.

H.J. Habakkuk, *American and British Technology in the Nineteenth Century; the Search for Labour-Saving Inventions*. Cambridge, UK: Cambridge University Press, 1962.

Robert Hendrickson, *The Road to Appomattox*. New York: J. Wiley, 1998.

Christopher Hibbert, *Queen Victoria: A Personal History*. Cambridge, MA: De Capo, 2000.

Richard Hofstadter, *The American Political Tradition*. New York: Knopf, 1973.

Paul Israel, *Edison: A Life of Invention*. New York: J. Wiley, 1998.

Lawrence James, *Raj: The Making and Unmaking of British India.* New York: St. Martin's/Griffin, 1997.

Barbara Jelavich, *History of the Balkans.* 2 vols. New York: Cambridge University Press, 1983.

Eugene Kamenka, ed., *The Portable Karl Marx.* New York: Viking Press, 1983.

Henryk Katz, *The Emancipation of Labor: A History of the First International.* New York: Greenwood Press, 1992.

Paul M. Kennedy, *The Rise of the Anglo-German Antagonism, 1860–1914.* London; Boston: Allen & Unwin, 1980.

Walther Kirchner, *Western Civilization from 1500.* New York: Harper Perennial, 1991.

Lionel Kochan and Richard Abraham, *The Making of Modern Russia.* London: Macmillan Press, 1983.

Peter Kolchin, *Unfree Labor: American Slavery and Russian Serfdom.* Cambridge, MA: Harvard University Press, 1987.

Ferdinand Lesseps, *The History of the Suez Canal: A Personal Narrative.* Edinburgh, Scotland: William Blackwood and Sons, 1876.

Albert S. Lindemann, *A History of European Socialism.* New Haven, CT: Yale University Press, 1984.

James A. MacKay, *Alexander Graham Bell: A Life.* New York: J. Wiley, 1998.

Karl Marx and Frederick Engels, *Manifesto of the Communist Party.* New York: International, 1983.

Karl Marx and V.I. Lenin, *The Civil War in France: The Paris Commune.* New York: International, 1988.

Stephen F. Mason, *History of the Sciences.* London: Routledge & Paul, 1953.

William S. McFeely, *Frederick Douglass.* New York: Norton, 1991.

Larry McMurtry, *Crazy Horse.* New York: Viking, 1999.

James M. McPherson, *Battle Cry of Freedom: The Civil War Era.* New York: Ballatine, 1989.

Samuel E. Morison, *The Oxford History of the American People.* New York: Oxford University Press, 1965.

Walter G. Moss, *Russia in the Age of Alexander II, Tolstoy, and Dostoevsky.* London: Anthem Press, 2002.

Anthony Nutting, *No End of a Lesson: The Story of Suez.* London: Constable, 1967.

Thomas Pakenham, *The Scramble for Africa, 1876–1912.* London: Weidenfeld and Nicolson, 1991.

Sir Bernard Pares, *A History of Russia.* New York: AMS Press, 1981.

Otto Pflanze, *Bismarck and the Development of Germany.* Princeton, NJ: Princeton University Press, 1990.

Alain Plessis, *The Rise and Fall of the Second Empire, 1852–1871.* Trans. Jonathan Mandelbaum. New York: Cambridge University Press, 1985.

Bernard Porter, *The Lion's Share: A Short History of British Imperialism, 1850–1970.* New York: Longman, 1996.

John Rewald, *The History of Impressionism.* New York: Museum of Modern Art, 1961.

Mark Ridley, *The Darwin Reader.* New York: Norton, 1996.

Burleigh Cushing Rodick, *Appomattox: The Last Campaign.* New York: Philosophical Library, 1965.

James H. Rubin, *Impressionism.* London: Phaidon, 1999.

Bertrand Russell, *A History of Western Philosophy.* New York: Simon & Schuster, 1959.

Tim Ryan and Bill Parham, *Colonial New Zealand Wars.* Wellington, New Zealand: Grantham House, 1986.

Carl Sandburg, *Abraham Lincoln.* New York: Harcourt, 1934.

William O. Taylor, *With Custer on the Little Bighorn: A Newly Discovered First Person Account.* New York: Viking, 1996.

Guy P.C. Thomson, *Patriotism, Politics, and Popular Liberalism in Nineteenth-Century Mexico: Juan Francisco Lucas and the Puebla Sierra.* Wilmington, DE: Scholarly Resources, 1999.

Robert C. Tucker, ed., *The Marx-Engels Reader.* New York: W.W. Norton, 1972.

Bruce Waller, *Bismarck.* New York: B. Blackwell, 1985.

Stanley Weintraub, *Victoria: An Intimate Biography.* New York: Dutton, 1987.

James Welch, *Killing Custer.* New York: W.W. Norton, 1994.

Neville Williams and Philip Waller, *Chronology of the Modern World, 1763–1992.* Oxford: Helicon, 1994.

Raymond Williams, *Culture and Society, 1780–1950.* New York: Columbia University Press, 1983.

George M. Wilson, *Patriots and Redeemers in Japan: Motives in the Meiji Restoration.* Chicago: University of Chicago Press, 1992.

Jay Winik, *April 1865: The Month That Saved America.* New York: HarperCollins 2001.

INDEX